Mountain Biking the Hawaiian Islands

Mauka to Makai

SECOND Edition

John Alford

'Ohana Publishing

Mountain Biking the Hawaiian Islands
Mauka to Makai
FIRST Edition - 1997
SECOND Edition - December 2000
1st Revision - June 2002

Written and produced by John Alford - 'Ohana Publishing
Production consulting by Blair Thorndike
DEM Maps (Golden Software/Surfer®) by David Amann
Illustrations by Curt Evans
Front cover photo credit - Kai Osorio (Maunawili Trail, O'ahu)
Back cover photo credit - Shar Sylva (Waikoloa, Hawai'i)
All photographs by John Alford, unless otherwise noted.

For additional information, contact:
'Ohana Publishing
P.O. Box 240170
Honolulu, HI. 96824-0170
toll free (877) MTB-RIDE
email: john@bikehawaii.com
www.bikehawaii.com

Library of Congress Catalog Card Number 00-091396
ISBN 0-9649843-2-6
Product of Hawai'i

"*E 'oni wale no 'oukou I ku'u pono, 'a'ole pau.*"
"Endless is the good that I have given to you to enjoy."
King Kamehameha I

Acknowledgements

From the Heart

This page is dedicated to the businesses and friends whose generosity and support have made this book possible.

Mahalo to friends and computer specialists David Amann for the map designs and Blair Thorndike for production. Also, a warm and sincere mahalo to John Clark for editing. Thanks to Curt Evans of Down/Up for the illustrations.

Mahalo to my sponsors, Bryan Klum & "Sam" Hoffman of Outrigger Hotels of Hawai'i for the styling hotels and condos, and for supporting the sport of mountain biking here in Hawai'i. A sincere mahalo to Jacob Heilbron and Pat White of Kona Mountain Bikes who generously contributed to this project and strongly support trail preservation in Hawai'i and across the globe.

Special thanks to Sam Hall (The Steady Wrench) and Scott Chaney (The Bike Shop) for your support and professional service of my Kona Mountain Bike. Mahalo to Patrick Madison and Golden Software for the amazing Surfer® program that created the DEM maps. Thanks to CatEye cyclometers, whose dependable altimeter/odometer contributed to the detail and accuracy of each trail measurement.

Special thanks are also due to my riding partners, Kathy Sarns, Preston Maginis, David Amann, Sophia Hoskins, Greg Laliberte, Tyler Ralston, David Goodman, Kai Osorio, Ken Mackie, Mike Schwinn, Tracy Paiva, Paul Aurely, Pat Tosaki, Carl Brooks (BikeFactory, O'ahu), Randall Okada (The Bike Shop), Phillip Yee, Kevin Hotema, Les, Keith Nishimoto, Darren Broom, Grant Wise, Dwain Orion, Jana Lawhn, Skip, Scott Jackson, Shane O'neil (Extreme Sports Maui), Tom Armstrong (Maui Mountain Bike Club), Grant Mitchell (Mauna Kea Mountain Bikes, Hawai'i), Grant Miller (Hawaiian Pedals, Hawai'i), Brad Ball and Billy Vinton on Lana'i, Ted Kanemitsu, Reggie Petersen, Ruth Ann Becker, Li Wang (Becker Communications) and Phillip Kikukawa (Moloka'i Bicycle), Bob Nooney (Island Biker, Maui), Ryan Lester (South Maui Cycles), Joe McNerney and Carolyn Gery (Bicycle John's, Kaua'i), Bert Almeida, Chama Najera, Rick Beach, Spencer Coffman, Christine Eccleston, Melissa Suarez, Todd Melton and John Sargent (The Bike Doktor, Kaua'i). You all have patience beyond the word.

To all my dear friends that offered their help during my travels, mahalo to Henry and Colene Wong, Denny and Kimber Carhart, Doug Herkes, Tom and Anne Hoadley, Hans Kersting, and Scott and Jennifer Hay-Roe for your support and encouragement.

A special thanks to Mike McKenna in California for your assistance with the "Mac". Thanks to National Park Service, Division of Forestry and Wildlife, and Twain Newhart for the fabulous photos. Special thanks to the State Department of Land and Natural Resources, Division of Forestry and Wildlife, Na Ala Hele's Curt Cottrell and Aaron Lowe of Oʻahu, Mark Peyton of Maui County, Ed Petteys and Craig Koga of Kauaʻi and Rod Oshiro and Pat Thiele of the Big Island of Hawaiʻi. Mahalo to Mardie Lane of Hawaiʻi Volcanoes National Park and Dianne Quitiquit of Parker Ranch. Also, to Lanaʻi Land Company. Thanks to Betsy Gagne and Randy Kennedy of the State Natural Area Reserves Commission for their valuable time and wealth of information.

To my mother and father, bless you both for loving each other and deciding to raise a family here in Hawaiʻi. Thanks for teaching me the values of the great outdoors and to respect mother earth. To my brothers, Kenny and Tom, and my sister, Nancy, thank you for your love and encouragement.

Finally, I thank God for granting me the fortitude to complete this project. And last of all, to my Kona Mountain Bike: thanks for the ride! Mahalo to all, from the heart. ©

Dedicated to my mother and father.

Contents

Foreword

Aloha! *Mountain Biking the Hawaiian Islands* is a comprehensive look at mountain biking island-wide from a bikers perspective. This book lists only the accessible trails open to mountain bikes by the State of Hawai'i's Division of Forestry and Wildlife, Hawai'i State Parks and Hawai'i Volcanoes National Park. It also includes a list of tour operators and some private pastures that may be ridden with approval from the land owners.

Since I began to write about Hawai'i's mountain biking trails during the spring of 1995, I have discovered beautiful biking routes. After the release of my second book in 1997, I began conducting my own bike tours under the name Bike Hawaii. In these pages you will find information on Bike Hawaii adventures, as well as other quality bike tour operators here in the islands. I encourage visiting riders to take full advantage of the various tours being offered.

Along with the digital elevation maps and trail descriptions, you will find important information on trail safety, etiquette and preservation. Riders are encouraged to pay attention to the facts about our islands' fragile environment. With this information in mind while using these trails, we can help preserve them for future generations.

Mountain biking has become increasingly popular here in Hawai'i, and it is time that all of us who ride on the public trails recognize that it is a privilege.

All of our trails are unique and deserve our utmost respect and consideration. We need to educate other trail users, as well as the abusers, so that restrictions will not be placed against mountain biking on Hawaiian trails. I hope that with the information contained in this book, we can all work together to be a part of the solution and not the problem. It is the true "Aloha Spirit" that has inspired me to share this information with you, my fellow off-road enthusiasts. Together we can all create a world of shared trail use that works for everyone.

Interpretation of information

The information in this guide is my interpretation of the listed trails' terrain, environment and accessibility. The distances and elevations of the trails were calculated from a CatEye CC-AT100 cyclocomputer with altimeter. However, allow some room for errors. The mileages shown on the maps are only estimates. It is your responsibility to use your own judgement and common sense when riding on these trails.

The following trail ratings were developed to help you select trails that match your riding ability. Riders are expected to meet these minimum requirements when choosing a prospective ride. From beginner to advanced, a riders endurance skills are expected to increase along with his or her technical expertise. Walking or carrying your bike is necessary on sections of almost every trail.

Beginner Riders:

Persons who have general knowledge of bicycling. Before going off-road, they should be competent in basic skills such as balancing well, stopping, starting, turning, shifting and braking. Beginners must expect bumpy and uneven terrain as common ground for mountain biking. Beginners should be able to handle mild uphill and downhill grades. If they encounter sections of trail that are beyond their skill level, they should dismount and walk their bikes.

Intermediate Riders:

Persons who have experience riding on 4-wheel drive roads and narrow single track. They should be competent in skills such as balancing well on steep uphill and downhill starts and stops, and be able to negotiate a variety of difficult and technical terrain. Intermediate riders should also be capable of enduring a wide variety of steep ascents and descents over miles of terrain.

Advanced Riders:

Persons who have exceptional judgement, balance and coordination on a bike. Riders are expected to be competent in technical riding skills such as, bunny hopping, doing drop-offs, wheeling and negotiating very difficult and technical terrain. Advanced riders are expected to meet the demands of challenging arduous uphill climbs for extended periods of time, and skillfully negotiating steep and treacherous downhills.

Special note to mountain bikers: DO NOT venture off trails or make your own short cuts. Mountain biking the trails of Hawai'i is a unique privilege and requires your utmost respect of the environment. Skidding your rear wheel is very destructive to the trail and should be avoided as much as possible. Do not move or disturb any of the natural resources, especially at historical native Hawaiian sites. Do your part to preserve and protect our natural environment and exercise proper riding techniques to minimize impact. Many trails are also used for hiking, and riders should be courteous to other trail users. Be cautious of recreational vehicles and never spook animals. Do not ride at excessive speeds when visibility is poor and stay off single track when it's wet or raining. Help ensure that our trails are kept open to all users and educate your fellow riders in regard to trail preservation and riding etiquette.

Warning: This guide is strictly informational. It is intended to show you where to gain trail access, and to give you an idea of what to expect. However, weather and erosion may change the trail conditions, creating situations that may exceed your riding abilities. Use these trails at your own risk and always wear protective gear when bicycling.

1 Mountain Biking in Hawai'i

From mauka to makai (the "mountains to the ocean"), *Mountain Biking the Hawaiian Islands* offers some of the most beautiful tropical riding in the world! Protected by thousands of miles of ocean, Hawai'i is known for its lush forests, sandy beaches and active volcanoes.

While there are many scenic road rides through plantation villages and historic Hawaiian cities, this guide focuses on fun and challenging off-road adventures for riders of all skill levels.

Nowhere else in the world can you mountain bike near a hot, steaming volcano while gazing out over a 400 foot deep volcanic caldera. Then, switch gears to enter a cool, misty tropical forest with awesome serpentine single track and fire-break roads. Tiny native birds flutter about and sing in the 'ohia trees. Pedal the acclivity to the summit of a 13,796 foot snow capped volcano, then coast down to a white sandy beach and mingle with the dolphins in the warm blue Pacific Ocean.

Take a few days and spend some quality time on each island. Have fun and enjoy the splendor of our island wonderland. When mountain biking the Hawaiian Islands, stop on occasion to enjoy the views of our tropical landscape, and don't forget your camera. These trails are all picture perfect.

Trail access - public or private

Here in the islands, a variety of public state trails are open to hikers and mountain bikers alike, none of which require a permit. Each trail is unique in its own way and differs in terrain, weather, and altitude. While some islands offer miles of single track, others have mostly dirt roads. All of the state trails are designated for hiking, and mountain bikers should expect to see backpackers, day-hikers and families with small children on the trails.

Several non-profit cycling clubs and bike stores offer organized rides and/or guided tours that cater to mountain bikers with all levels of experience. Most of the club rides are free and riders are encouraged to contact them to find out about current riding schedules. Private companies normally charge a fee and conduct their off-road tours and adventures on leased land or private property. However, commercial mountain bike tours on State Forestry land require a Commercial Trail Tour Activity permit and riders are urged not to support unofficial off-road tours on public land. A list of bike tours, bike clubs and bike stores, is included in the Appendix.

Riders may choose from the chilly alpine riding of up country Maui to the warm coastal roads of Lana'i. Or, pedal to the summit of Mauna Kea on the island of Hawai'i and experience high elevation snow biking during our winter months. Be sure to ride the many miles of hidden single track on the island of O'ahu. Don't miss the lush rainforest of Kamakou on Moloka'i or the many ridges and valleys of Koke'e on the island of Kaua'i. *Mountain Biking the Hawaiian Islands* is sure to satisfy even the most hungry of appetites for off-road pleasure.

Of the one million malihini (visitors) that arrive in Hawai'i every year, relatively few get to experience our mountainous ridges, valleys, streams and waterfalls. If this inspires the very outdoor person in you, I suggest you gear up and get riding. The trails of Hawai'i have so much to offer.

Many state trails border private property, and riders should observe and respect posted signs. Many property owners have a difficult time keeping hikers and bikers off their land. Riders should respect "No Trespassing" or "Kapu" signs and ride only where access is permitted. Some private land

Respect No Trespassing signs.
Ride on open trails only.

owners allow recreational access on their property, but usually by special permission only. Certain landowners or lessees charge a fee, while others may require insurance and indemnification by having you sign a release. Know where you are riding and if access is permitted, whether it be in Hawai'i or elsewhere. Trespassing is illegal and prosecution by the government or by the land owner is a possibility.

This guide will introduce you to the trails that are accessible and open to mountain bikes. If permits are necessary, the individual trail descriptions will tell you how to to obtain them. Calling ahead is recommended to ensure permits are still available. Check Permit Information at the back of the book for local phone numbers.

Most of the trails in this guide are managed by Na Ala Hele Hawai'i Trail and Access System, which falls under the Hawai'i State Department of Land and Natural Resources (DLNR) and the Division of Forestry and Wildlife (DOFAW). Na Ala Hele currently manages hundreds of miles of Hawai'i trails and accesses. Hawai'i's state parks and even its national parks allow the privilege of some mountain biking within their jurisdictions. Other trails may fall under the Natural Area Reserves System (NARS), which protects endangered native Hawaiian plants and animals.

NAH sign indicating a multi-use trail.

Some trails, such as Tantalus, Pahole and Helemano on O'ahu, have been restricted to mountain bikes for different reasons. NARS suggests restrictions for the protection and preservation of endangered native Hawaiian species of plant and animal life. DLNR suggests "rest periods" when certain trails receive too much impact as a result of high usage.

The Tantalus trail complex was temporarily placed off-limits to mountain bike use by DLNR in early 1996 as an attempt to rest the trails during the winter rainy season. With the help of various DOFAW volunteers and outside groups such as Hawaiʻi Mountain Bike Advisory Committee (HMBAC) and the Hawaiʻi Bicycling League (HBL), numerous hours were spent restoring areas of the trail to withstand the volume of shared use. During the summer of 1996, Tantalus showed major signs of improvement. However, plans to re-open certain trails within the Tantalus complex are still being evaluated.

Future partial or total trail closures to mountain bikes are not just rumors. Similar restrictions have already occurred in many mainland states in recent years. Aggressive riding styles should be saved for races and 4WD roads, not for precious single track. Get educated on our current situation and help protect what we still have. Always observe trail signs and respect the ʻaina (land).

Enjoy and preserve Hawaiian single track!

Commuting

The mountain bike has become a part of recreation and transportation for millions of Americans since its birth in the early 1980's. When using the bike on trails as it was designed for, a rider will experience endless hours of off-road thrills and sometimes spills. Today, the mountain bike is also used as a utilitarian mode of transportation on paved roads. From bicycle couriers to law enforcement, the mountain bike has proved worthy as a primary main source of reliable transportation for workers, as well as weekend riders. The Honolulu Police Department continues to expand their Bicycle Detail units to enforce the law while in the saddle. Security personnel from various businesses, hospitals and school campuses also utilize mountain bikes to get into and around busy and congested areas faster, helping to minimize response time to emergency calls.

Commuting on Hawai'i's roadways via bicycle has also become increasingly popular. Many people use their bicycles as transportation to get to and from work, ultimately helping to decrease the number of vehicles on our highways. Road riders often prefer mountain bikes over road bikes because they can be used on and off the road.

Many riders use their mountain bike as their sole piece of transportation and ride to and from the trail head. In many cases, the road rides between trail destinations are possible, but not practical. The State Department of Transportation has put some effort into improving our shared roadways and creating more bicycle lanes, but the riding conditions of our highways are still poor. Many of our paved roads and highways are narrow and have winding turns. Most of our roads are shared roadways and facilitate motor vehicles and large trucks. Be very careful when riding the highways of Hawai'i. If the distance between you and the trail is far, drive a car to the trail head. Check the specific island map included in this guide to estimate the distance.

If you choose to road ride, always ride with the flow of traffic and wear bright colored clothing. If you ride at night, use reflectors and a bright light to make you more visible.

Bike lanes are designated for the preferential or exclusive use of bicycles and are marked with signs and paint striping. Remember that bike lanes are only separated from moving traffic by a painted line, so use caution. Do not "ride the line". Cyclists are encouraged to remain alert and stay to the far right of the bike lane or shoulder.

Beginner riders are encouraged to learn bicycling basics and techniques in open areas such as parks or on a bike path, which is a separated right-of-way from traffic.

On O'ahu, the public bus system provides passengers a front loading bike rack on most routes, capable of carrying two bicycles at no extra charge. This has proved helpful for commuters who may use their bikes to get around town, but live too far away to ride into town and back. For a detailed schedule of routes and times, contact TheBus at 848-5555.

Night riding

As the warm Hawaiian sun sinks deep into the western horizon, darkness falls on our island chain and the environment takes on a whole new perspective. Our island's valleys, ridges and coastlines are quite beautiful at night and provide opportunities for nocturnal recreation. Just as some scuba divers explore the ocean depths at night, some mountain bikers enjoy the thrill of night riding. Imagine, no crowds and no sunburn. Just the challenge of staying on your bike without falling. On a clear night, a full Hawaiian moon may provide enough natural light to ride many of the dirt roads.

Off-road night riding is a possibility on some trails. Four wheel drive roads are recommended over narrow single track, providing night riders with safer and wider riding areas. Single track can also be fun at night, but should only be attempted by advanced riders with knowledge of that particular trail. Roots, rocks and cliff areas can be visually deceiving at night and riders should use extra caution, especially if the ground is wet. To ensure safety, riders should

always stay together and not separate from the group.

Dual beam light systems are recommended to facilitate brighter flood lighting when needed. Some bike lights are not designed for trail illumination and are usually the ones that require disposable batteries. These lighting systems are designed for visibility by traffic and not for off roading.

Night trail riders should utilize the highest quality lighting systems to light up the night. Of the many systems available, Nightsun® produces a lightweight, 45-watt rechargeable battery, dual beam system, featuring thermoplastic brushguards to help protect the lens from shock and debris. With dual beam systems, utilize the low beam in most situations to prolong battery life and the high beam only when needed, such as for sections of trail which are rough and for areas where you might pick up speed. When used sparingly, the ni-cad battery can provide three to four hours of night riding fun.

A good addition to a handle bar mounted light is a helmet mounted light. When combining the two, you get trail illumination along with directional lighting from your helmet. The more light, the better, however, there is no replacement for the sun. Whenever off-roading at night, use extreme caution and never attempt dangerous cliff areas or reach speeds that you normally would during daylight hours. Also plan to carry a flashlight, in the event your light fails or is damaged in a fall.

Depending on what side of the island you decide to ride, it is recommended to factor in the rise or setting of the sun. The colors of either time of day are fascinating from the trail looking seaward to the horizon. While sunrises are a bit more difficult to time because of the early riding time, the setting sun makes for a perfect beginning for a night ride. Equally spectacular is the rising of the full moon, making for a mysterious ride along the dark and eerie trails and dirt roads.

For those who have not yet explored night riding, a whole new world of night time opportunity awaits you amidst the darkness of these islands.

2 The Environment
Hawaiian weather

Hawai'i's mild climate attracts visitors from around the globe. Being on an island in the middle of the Pacific usually means year 'round warm weather and sunshine, but because of the extreme elevations found in the Hawaiian Islands, the climate in some areas can change rapidly and sometimes with severe effects.

Maui's Haleakala rises skyward some 10,023 feet while Hawai'i's Mauna Loa and Mauna Kea are both over 13,000 feet. Snowcapped during the winter months, temperatures drop below zero degrees fahrenheit, often with a dangerous wind chill factor. During storms, high winds and rain are common on the lower slopes, while icy blizzards may cover the summits.

When planning a journey up mauka, dress accordingly and check the local weather forecast. You can call the summit report on the island of Maui or Hawai'i. Phone numbers are located in the Appendix.

The tropical weather of Hawai'i usually calls for sunshine with occasional showers in the windward and mauka regions. During the winter months, temperatures may drop into the low 60's, but 85 degree days are not uncommon. A decrease of 2 to 4 degrees for every 1,000 foot elevation is a good way to estimate the temperature at higher elevations. It is a good idea to carry warm clothes if you are planning a ride to higher elevations.

Hawai'i's rainfall is more prevalent during the months of October to April. Our rains are usually short bursts and seldom last for days at a time. The higher elevations and windward sides of our mountain ranges usually see more precipitation. Sometimes, we experience sunshine with a warm gentle rain that cools the heat of the day. This is referred to as "Liquid Sunshine". Keep in mind, if you get caught in a rainstorm while biking, the roads and trails will become very slippery. Wet roots and rocks can cause quick unexpected falls.

During heavy rain, be cautious near river beds. Flash flooding can occur, even when the rain doesn't appear to be strong. The summit above may be raining much harder than where you are and a sudden downpour may be all it takes to create powerful changes in stream flow and water levels.

Our normal northeasterly winds are referred to as "trade winds". Usually steady, these winds cool the heat of the day and help rid the island of air pollution. The trade winds are refreshing and even more enjoyable when working up a sweat.

"Kona" weather is uncomfortable and occurs when hot and humid south winds blow. Sometimes Kona winds carry a volcanic haze (aka: Vog) from the Big Island of Hawai'i and can carry it as far as Kaua'i. Then the horizon becomes lost in a haze of gray, and you'll drip with perspiration, even when just relaxing. Kona weather is most common between the months of October and April.

On the island of Hawai'i where molten lava meets the sea, dangerous steam clouds full of toxic gases can create a hydrochloric "acid rain" down wind from the source. This can be seriously dangerous to eyes and lungs. To avoid exposure, check with park rangers about current hazards and conditions. Learn more about the volcano in the chapter "Hawai'i - The Big Island".

In the absence of trade winds or storms, diurnal heating and cooling of the islands bring light on-shore breezes during the day that switch to off-shore breezes during the night.

The most severe weather in the islands is brought on by hurricanes. From the months of June through November, all eyes are on the satellite maps of the Pacific, watching storms that may build into full blown hurricanes. Hurricanes bring extremely high storm surges, huge surf and powerful winds. Thanks to our highly sophisticated weather warning system and our State Civil Defense, we always receive hurricane warnings far in advance.

Sunscreen is a must, especially for those of us with "fair skin". A Skin Protection Factor SPF of 30+ is highly recommended. The sun's rays are strongest between 10 a.m. and 2 p.m. If at all possible, try to ride before and after this period of high ultra-violet ray intensity. If it is a cloudy day, still use sunscreen because the penetrating ultra violet rays can still burn your skin. Wear a hat and a shirt and lather up with a good non-greasy, sweat-proof sunblock.

To avoid dehydration, drink plenty of water and carry extra water with you during your ride. Refer to the "Hydration and Nutrition" and the "Before you ride" sections for a good planner.

Hawai'i's flora and fauna

Along our trails, you will encounter many different types of flora and fauna, most of which will not be native. Much of the Hawaiian rainforest is now inundated with many foreign species of vegetation. Hawai'i ranks highest for the most endangered species on the planet. Certain valleys and ridgelines have been designated as a Natural Area Reserve System (NARS) or Water Shed Conservation District to help protect the declining natural environment. The pristine tropical forests and coastal areas of our islands are home to many species of life that depend on the ecosystem for survival. The chain of events that take place when foreign species are introduced can seriously alter the natural habitats. Listed below are just a few of the species commonly seen.

Our official state tree, the kukui (candlenut tree) with its distinctive light green foliage, is commonly found growing in our lush, green valleys. Introduced by early Polynesians, the kukui has been used by Hawaiians for hundreds of years. The kukui nut is very oily and burns quite easily. In days of old Hawai'i, the oil was used to fuel stone lamps, hence its English name candlenut. The nuts are sometimes dried, peeled, polished and strung as leis. Some folks dry roast the nuts and use them as a relish with salt and pepper. Do not mistake these nuts for macadamia nuts. The kukui is a very powerful laxative.

Native koa acacia, known for it's beautiful woodgrain is harvested for use as wooden furnishings such as, bowls, utensils, jewelry and even canoes. It is seen up mauka and is easily spotted along certain trails with its sickle shaped phyllodes (leaf stems).

The dry, coastal regions commonly have an abundance of haole koa and kiawe. The haole koa is a wild bush that grows rampant and is considered to be a weed. It is a distant relative of the native koa tree. The kiawe tree has a hard wood which is used often in outdoor barbeques to flavor the smoke. The kiawe also has small branches that fall from the tree and are covered with hundreds of small, sharp thorns. These pesky thorns are known for giving cyclists multiple tire punctures in just one pass. Read the section on Bicycle Maintenance for tips on how to protect your tires from the wrath of the kiawe.

'Ohi'a is one of the dominant native trees found on our mountain trails. The 'ohi'a lehua blossoms come in a variety of colors including red, orange and pale yellow. Legend says, if you pick these flowers, rains will soon follow.

A wide variety of ferns are also found along the trails. The obvious ground cover on most of our trails is the poky and stem laced false staghorn fern (uluhe). If you are wearing shorts and have to blaze through a patch of overgrown uluhe, be prepared for scratches on your legs.

A variety of introduced ginger plants are found along trails in wetter areas. The yellow and white ginger are the only ones with fragrant blossoms. Shampoo ginger or 'awapuhi kuahiwi was introduced by early Polynesians. The soapy juice squeezed from its buds is still used as a shampoo by campers.

A wide variety of edible fruits are found along the trails. The introduced guava and strawberry guava are the most common. Mountain apples, mangoes, bananas, star fruit, lilikoi (passion fruit) and the native 'ohelo berries are also found on cer-

What a pig! photo: DOFAW

tain trails. Never pick and eat unknown fruit.

The hapu'u is a tree fern which grows a fibrous and golden hairy trunk. Fiddleheads are the developing young fronds which look like a monkey's tale when first sprouting. Slowly unfurling into a beautiful arching green frond, the endemic hapu'u is a photogenic gift of nature. Unfortunately, these beautiful tree ferns get pushed over and their starchy pith is eaten by destructive feral pigs (pua'a).

Up mauka, the feral pig is one of our more common wild animals. First introduced by early Polynesian voyagers, the pigs' destructive habits have threatened our Hawaiian rainforests for years. Pigs trample plants and eat the ferns and important undergrowth which holds the top soil in place. The wild boars have tusks, and if cornered or frightened may charge at the threat, but it is highly unlikely that you will ever get this close to a wild pig. They are quick to run when they see or hear people.

Wild goats, are sometimes seen from a distance clinging to steep and dangerous cliff areas. When at the base of a valley wall, you must be aware of goats above you. Sometimes they kick loose rocks and cause them to fall.

Some of the favorite game for hunters are axis deer, pigs, goats and some fowl, such as ring neck pheasant, erckel's francolin, quail and wild turkeys. Each island is diverse in its hunting and seasons. Because of the popular hunting areas that co-exist in the same mountains that we hike and bike in, it is important to your safety to stay on the main trail and observe signs.

Wild goats. photo: DOFAW

The mongoose is a small fury animal which

looks like a weasel. Sometimes you'll see one running from shrub to shrub as if playing hide and seek. These little critters, often seen as roadkill, have grown in numbers since their introduction some years ago. The mongoose was supposed to help control our rat population. Unfortunately,

Pesky mongoose. photo: DOFAW

rats are nocturnal and the mongoose is not. Now, the mongoose is a problem for our birdlife. In particular, they prey on ground nesting birds and their eggs.

Despite the remoteness of our islands, and Department of Agriculture laws, illegal reptiles and other foreign species continue to make their way to Hawai'i. Many are smuggled in by new residents. Others, such as the brown tree snake, sometimes hitch rides in the wheel wells of planes arriving from foreign places. The introduction of foreign species poses a serious threat to native Hawaiian plants and animals.

Along coastal trails, riders must exercise caution in the event that they encounter an endangered species such as the green sea turtle (honu), or the Hawaiian monk seal ('Ilio holo i ka uaua). The Natural Area Reserves System (NARS) protects these and other species such as the Laysan albatross that nests along coastal trails. The nesting areas sought by the birds usually have low visitor volume and long runways necessary for their take-offs. It is vital that you adhere to the rules of the NARS where riding bikes is strictly prohibited.

Hawai'i's little critters known to sting and bite include bees, wasps, red ants, centipedes, scorpions, brown recluse spiders, black widow spiders and mosquitoes. With the

Axis fawn. photo: DOFAW

Laysan Albatross in flight. photo: DOFAW

exception of the mosquito, most of the biting or stinging critters are found in the lower, drier regions. Check the ground beneath you before sitting down to avoid getting goosed by one of these pests.

Mosquitoes and fruit gnats are most prevalent in moist and windless areas. A good splash of repellent should help to keep these pests away. Cockroaches live almost everywhere and while not threatening, are a nuisance. Keep food sealed to avoid sharing your meals with uninvited guests.

Some small leeches have been found in the sugar cane flumes. Swimming in these flumes is not recommended, not only because of leeches, but also because of possible fertilizer, pesticide or bacterial contamination in the water. Leptospirosis is a bacteria sometimes found in trace amounts in mountain streams. If infected through an open cut or mucous membrane, the illness can mimic flu symptoms. If in doubt, consult your doctor.

One of the biggest concerns for mountain bikers is bees. Typically, our trails have fragrant flowers which bees like to snack on. If you are allergic to stings, you should carry your antihistamine and anaphylactic kit as prescribed by your doctor, just in case. Refer to References to find out more about our native plants and animals.

Resting Hawaiian monk seals.
photo: DOFAW

Trail Preservation Education

It is imperative that we learn how to share the trails. Educating ourselves about trail erosion is a good start. Learning riding techniques to minimize impacts on the environment will help preserve the resources and promote shared trail access.

The mountain bike community has grown tenfold since its introduction in the early 1980's. Bike technology is changing so rapidly that most models are outdated within a year. The skill levels of some riders have also gone into a higher dimension. Top riders are performing maneuvers and tricks that were only dreamed about 10 years ago. With this advancement in technology and riding, it is time for biking etiquette to move forward, too.

Mountain biking the trails of Hawai'i is a unique privilege. We are blessed to be able to ride some of the most beautiful single track in the world. This is a joy that only a relative few can experience. To preserve that privilege, we need to care for the natural environment. As a biker, it is your responsibility to learn the techniques to minimize impacts on the trails.

Responsible riding means to think before you act. Single track are not the place to be when conditions are wet. The tearing action of a skidding bicycle tire on a wet trail expedites the erosion process.

Certain sections of low-lying trails trap and hold water, making mud holes long after the rains have fallen. Riders should dismount and carry their bikes around these areas. Riding through mud puddles will only make the problem worse.

During wet and rainy weather, select a trail that can handle it. Four-wheel drive roads are the only recommended rides on wet days. This guide will identify these roads that are accessible during wet weather. Single track are precious, and riders should stay on the main trail. Making short cuts kill the vegetation and add to erosion. Acts of irresponsible riding also promote a negative image for mountain biking and can lead to increased trail maintenance and/or trail closure.

If you see other trail users such as hikers, other bikers or equestrians, greet them and slow or stop to allow for safe passing. Some of the cliff areas are dangerous and a reckless pass can be frightening and hazardous for everyone on the trail.

All mountain bikers should follow the International Mountain Bicycling Association's (IMBA) six rules of the trail:

1. Ride on open trails only.
2. Leave no trace.
3. Control your bicycle.
4. Always yield trail.
5. Never scare animals.
6. Plan ahead.

Another way of preserving the trail is not to litter. Pack out what you pack in. Show some Aloha 'Aina ("love of the land"). If you come across other people's trash, pick it up and pack it out if you have the extra space. Do not bury your trash. Local mountain critters will dig it up and make a mess. If you have to smoke, be extremely cautious near dry forests or grass, and always bring your butts home.

Another way to preserve the environment is to remove "hitch hikers" (foreign seeds from unwanted plants and weeds) from your clothes. Contamination of native forests with foreign seeds from other countries or even local trails poses a serious threat to our fragile ecosystems. Do your part and clean the dirt and debris off your socks, shoes and bike before exploring your next trail. This will dramatically decrease the chances of spreading unwanted vegetation.

Given the opportunity to ride these trails, you should use them wisely. It is to everyone's advantage to know the facts and respect the land. Educate your fellow bikers. It is our responsibility to stop our friends from careless and destructive use of the trails.

Various organizations are popping up world-wide to help educate and support mountain biking by promoting responsible riding and trail preservation. Probably the largest is the International Mountain Biking Association (IMBA). Formed in 1988, IMBA continues to be a successful advocate for the sport of mountain biking and has helped to reopen closed trails in many mainland states.

On a local level, Hawai'i has its own success story. Hawai'i Bicycling League (HBL), established in the 1960s, has been our advocate for all aspects of bicycling. HBL's administration now plays an important role as an advocate for mountain biking as well. In 1989, HBL, in cooperation with the State of Hawai'i Department of Education formed a program called "BikeEd." BikeEd has become part of the elementary school curriculum for 4th graders. The students are taught general biking techniques, traffic laws and safety. Equipped with helmets and bikes, they have five 45 minute sessions with three certified instructors.

Educational programs for children like this one are important for the future of mountain biking. Teaching today's cyclists common sense and the importance of responsible riding will keep our trails open and safe for future generations to enjoy.

For more on local bike clubs, refer to the Club Rides section listed under each island chapter.

Tread lightly

Damage to trails caused by erosion and accelerated by mountain bikers is usually confined to certain fragile sections, such as steep hills and various puddling areas. In these sections of trail, proper riding techniques will help minimize impact.

One of the essential riding techniques is for you to always be in control of your bike, and to maintain traction on the trail. Nobby tires are designed to hold firm on unpaved surfaces and are a must for mountain bikes. As long as your tires don't lose traction and the terrain is dry, erosion will be held to a bare minimum.

When you encounter man-made steps, dismount and carry your bike over them. The impact caused from riding down makeshift steps loosens them and creates unneeded additional trail maintenance.

Knowing the stopping distance of your bike is especially important when going down a steep hill. Skidding or sliding will cause the tire to tear at the surface soil and increase erosion. On steep sections of trail, a skidding bicycle tire wears down the surface, eventually creating a small rut. Rains will enlarge the rut when water runoff funnels down it. If the rut is not filled, the trail will become increasingly damaged by additional rain and other trail users. To avoid skidding, use both the front and rear brakes together and lean back to keep your weight over the rear wheel. If the hill is too steep, dismount and walk your bike down it. When accelerating or climbing a hill, again keep your weight over the rear wheel and stay in a higher gear to prevent loss of traction. Up-shifting into a higher gear makes it a little harder to pedal, but will help keep your rear wheel from spinning out during acceleration.

Puddles caused by poor drainage will remain long after the rain. Riding or stomping through these areas makes things worse. When you encounter a mud puddle, dismount and carefully hike your bike around the puddled area to prevent further damage, but try not to trample the vegetation.

Proper riding techniques also include controlling your speed. Besides increasing your stopping distance and risk, speed can loosen roots and rocks that help to hold the soil in place. Speed may threaten your safety and the safety of other trail users. When visibility is poor, such as at turns and in dark areas of a trail, slow down and travel at a low speed so you can stop quickly, if necessary.

If we all ride safely, preserve trails and help to reduce user conflicts, mountain bikers will be welcomed and closed trails may be reopened for everyone to enjoy. With this in mind, ride with a smile and help educate others with your positive attitude and knowledge.

Walk your bike at muddy sections of trail.

Getting involved in trail maintenance

Before a trail is made, raw forest, dense vegetation and steep grades are the norm. Before the first tree is cut, many days of research are spent to determine the environmental impact of a proposed trail. State conservationists conduct environmental and archaeological assessments, while botanists inspect the area for rare and endangered species. Once a trail is approved, a team of volunteers and a handful of paid personnel begin cutting away vegetation for the new trail. That task alone sometimes takes years to complete. Volunteer trail crews finish their day's work with blisters, sunburn and exhaustion, but with a feeling of great accomplishment. The men and women who volunteer their time to blaze the trails that we bike on are dedicated people who enjoy what they are doing. Some are busy executives while others retirees. In some cases, mainland visitors volunteer some of their vacation time just to lend a helping hand and have a chance to experience our wilderness from a different perspective. Hikers and mountain bikers alike are encouraged to get involved in trail building and maintenance to help ensure that our trails are safe and enjoyable for everyone.

The Hawai'i Mountain Bike Advisory Committee (HMBAC), a division of the Hawai'i Bicycling League (HBL), organizes trail work projects on the island of O'ahu almost monthly. This attracts trail enthusiasts from cyclists to avid hikers. During 1998, in cooperative efforts with Hawai'i State Parks, HMBAC adopted the 'Aiea Loop Trail. Group efforts provided Hawai'i State Parks with over 400 volunteer hours laying gravel, weed whacking, and the construction of a natural rock ford. HMBAC was also awarded a $3,500. grant from the PowerBar D.I.R.T. program. Monies were used to purchase supplies and two recycled plastic trail side benches. Trail building tools were donated from IMBA and Rock Shox to assist the growing list of volunteers such as, Youth Conservation Corps (YCC), Youth for Environmental Services (YES), Honolulu Police Department Bicycle Detail, Boy Scouts of America, United States Marines Corps and numerous windsurfers, bikers and hikers.

On the island of Maui, DOFAW and Na Ala Hele with volunteers from the Maui Mountain Bike Club joined forces in a collaboration effort to improve trails in the Kula Forest Reserve at Polipoli. After completing the research for a proposed trail, the teams broke ground and began building the Mamane Trail. Na Ala Hele's Mike Baker and Tori Higashino, and Tom Armstrong of Maui Mountain

Bike Club spear-headed the project. Additional help was provided by the Youth Conservation Corps (YCC).

On the island of Hawai'i, the Big Island Mountain Bike Association (BIMBA) provides organized trail maintenance and group rides, and promotes safe and responsible mountain biking. Riders of all ages and skill levels often participate in the many activities that BIMBA coordinates. Organized efforts like this continue to help the states cost of trail repair and restores safer, user friendly trails for all to enjoy.

In recent years, Na Ala Hele has also encouraged a trail stewardship program where clubs, groups and private businesses can adopt and maintain a trail to support the state's effort. Trail maintenance can be expensive, and with a fluctuating state budget for trails and access, trail steward-

ship programs can be an effective way to keep trails open to mountain bikers and other trail users.

New trails are the most expensive and the hardest to complete. According to Na Ala Hele, the Maunawili Trail, on O'ahu's windward side, cost the state $50,000 to build. Over 1,000 Sierra Club volunteers spent three years to blaze seven miles of new trail. Depending on the difficulty of the terrain, approximately twenty volunteers moved at a pace of about 500 feet per day.

In addition, 200 United States Marines completed one mile in just three days. Yet, with all of this time and money, natural erosion began to take place from day one.

All trails suffer from natural erosion caused by rain, wind and water run off. Hikers, bikers and in some cases equestrians, accelerate the erosion process. Eroded problem areas of trails where water run-off is great and steep grades exist need constant maintenance. Overhead canopies of lush growth block out the drying effects of the sun and the trail retains the moisture.

Some of these areas have been improved by the addition of waterbars, man-made steps and/or boardwalks. Water bars are made from large tree branches, trunks or synthetic material and are placed diagonally across the trail, partially sunk into the ground. They direct water off the trail and slow bikers down. Some trails that have exceptionally steep terrain are modified with log steps that resemble waterbars. The steps are placed to minimize sliding by hikers and cyclists. Boardwalks have been constructed on certain areas of trails with poor drainage. Here the biker doesn't even touch the ground below. This has proven to be the most effective device to prevent further damage.

Maintenance is important in the quest to preserve trails and make them safe. The state and some private organizations continue to work together, giving people like us a chance to volunteer and be a part of the solution and not the problem. As a trail user, an opportunity to help maintain trails is one of the best ways to give something back to the community.

IMBA has compiled a list of literary resources for trail development and construction which is being used in Hawai'i to restore existing trails. Their illustrated book contains technical information on trail design for heavily used trails.

Wherever you live, you can make a difference by getting involved in trail maintenance. Contact your local bike clubs or forestry department for information on how you can help. See the Appendix for contact numbers.

Mountain Biking Safety Tips
Off-road hazards

The old saying, "Expect the unexpected" holds true even in the beauty of Hawai'i's outdoors. When you are mountain biking, you need to be aware of your surroundings and watch out for hikers and dangerous areas of the trail. Anytime you venture off the smooth asphalt onto a mountain trail, you will encounter a different set of hazards. Typically, roots, rocks and cliffs are the most common dangers. Watch the trail surface and keep an eye out for changes in terrain and protruding objects. Tree stumps and boulders are sometimes hidden among the shrubs and grass. If you were to accidentally catch one of these with your tire or pedal, you could be thrown from your bike. You know the saying, "It's not the fall that hurts you, it's that sudden stop." You should always be wearing safety gear, which is covered in the Safety Accessories section.

The weather can change rapidly, especially at the higher elevations of Maui and Hawai'i. A quick burst of rain will turn your trail surface into a slippery hazard. If you get caught in the rain, expect roots and rocks to become slick as ice. During heavy rains, stream levels can rise quickly and flood certain sections of trails. Flash floods can occur without warning and can be life-threatening. Use extreme caution near streams and waterfalls.

The water from the streams and puddles may contain leptospirosis and other harmful bacteria. Drinking stream water is not recommended unless it is treated, boiled or filtered with an adequate filtering device. Swimming or riding with open wounds can lead to infection and illness caused from leptospirosis. Contact the State Division of Forestry and Wildlife for further information.

Recreational vehicles are permitted on some roads and can be a hazard to bikers. Motorcycles, All Terrain Vehicles (ATV's) and 4WD trucks move fast. Never assume that they see you. Stay alert. Look and listen for approaching motorized vehicles and move out of their way.

Deep in our valleys, hunters roam the forests with crossbows and guns, searching for pigs and game birds. Bikers are advised to stay on the main trail to avoid entering a hunting zone.

Rock climbing

The volcanic rock in Hawai'i's mountains is a hazard for those who enjoy rock climbing. Our volcanic rock is brittle and crumbles easily. For your own safety, do not attempt to leave the safety of the trail to climb cliffs.

Getting lost

It does happen now and then to folks who leave the main trail and lose their sense of direction. The following tips should help you avoid becoming a lost mountain biker:

- Darkness sets in fast after sunset, so don't begin your mountain adventures late in the day.
- Stay on the main trail.
- Use a map and compass.
- Pack a mini-survival kit and carry a cellular phone and flashlight for emergencies.
- Never bike alone.

Safety accessories

Your bike has been built to withstand the stress of off-roading, and suspension can be added to diminish shock caused by bumps and uneven terrain. Padded saddles help to add comfort to your 'okole (butt) while riding and nobby tires improve traction on dirt and mud.

Given all the improvements we make to our bikes, it makes sense that we should improve our personal protection as well. Safety gear helps to prevent injury in case of accident. Experienced mountain bikers know that, "it's not if you fall, it's when you fall".

Wearing safety gear while mountain biking is a must. The highest priority is to protect your head. Find yourself a helmet that is comfortable and fits properly. Check for the ANSI or SNELL labels that show the helmet has passed regulated safety specifications. Bell Helmets have been designing durable and functional helmets to protect the heads of off-road enthusiasts for years. From auto racing to mountain biking, you will find that Bell Helmets has a size and style that fits your every need, plus a warranty replacement program that is hard to beat. The Bell Fusion Series®, offers up to 28 ventilation holes to add free flowing air to cool your head and release the heat. Many other brands and styles are available. Have your local bike shop help select one that is right for you.

Goggles or sunglasses are helpful to protect your eyes. However, plastic sunglasses with a 100% UV rating will be safer than actual glass. In the event of impact to the face, glass could shatter and cause further injury. Flying insects, rocks, dirt, branches and even bright sunlight are hazards that eye protection helps to deal with. Oakley® designs performance eye protection for all sports. Mountain bikers use Oakley products because of style, fit and eye protection that you can count on. Ultra light, stress resistant frames with Plutonite® lens material provides the rider with comfort, durability and 100% U.V. protection. Oakley's sport line has a variety of styles and prices. See your local bike shop or sunglass authority for more information and new styles.

For the safety conscious rider, shin guards, elbow pads, knee pads and full face shields are additional equipment that further protection.

Selecting appropriate biking shoes is also important. Along with comfort and proper fit, your shoes must have nobby soles for traction. Some riders prefer hiking shoes while others choose specially designed biking shoes with a binding system. Never ride with slippers or sandals.

Wear your helmet!

Protect your chain rings from serious damage by using protection such as the Rock-Ring®. Flying rocks or direct impact when attempting to get over large obstacles can chip sprocket teeth and bend your chain rings. An easy-to-install Rock-Ring will help protect your chain rings from damage.

Safe riding tips

Safety should always be a major consideration in every sport, so consider the following before mountain biking. Along with wearing your protective safety gear, know your bike and familiarize yourself with its handling characteristics. Practice stopping, turning and shifting in both wet and dry conditions. When down shifting gears on an uphill, be sure not to apply too much pressure on the pedals during your shift. This can snap your chain or chip teeth on your chain ring and cogs. An early down shift just before a grade steepens or shifting while the bike still has momentum will remedy this. Stay seated while shifting to prevent an accident in case your chain slips and you miss the next gear. If this happens, you will experience a hyper-speed rotation of the the crank arm which could lead to a fall.

Adjusting your seat to the proper height for different terrain also aides in comfort and maneuverability. Your foot should rest flat on the pedal at the down stroke with only a slight bend of the knee. If you are riding a steep downhill or practicing your trials techniques, try dropping your seat lower and you'll find that your mobility on the bike increases.

When mountain biking on single track, stay on the trail. Always ride with a friend, and tell others where you are going and what time you're expected back. Don't make last minute changes to your plans without telling someone. In the unlikely event that you would need rescue assistance, rescue teams would find you much faster if they knew exactly where to look. Carry a cellular phone in case you need to call for help in an emergency. This safety feature has saved many and likely will save many more. If you have an emergency in a remote area, call 911 and ask for the fire department. They will activate their ground and air rescue personnel to assist you and call for an ambulance if one is needed.

Don't be a brave, "NO FEAR" type of off-road warrior unless you are willing to suffer the consequences. If an area of a trail looks too critical for your skill level, dismount and walk your bike. There are many steep cliffs on our trails, and you should always be cautious, especially if you are an amateur. Many of our trails are narrow single track, so ride with caution and don't take any unnecessary risks. Riding should be fun! Don't push yourself or your buddy to do anything that threatens your personal safety. Ride at speeds that match

the terrain and your skill level so that you can easily slow and stop if needed.

When you encounter other trail users such as hikers, equestrians or recreational vehicle drivers, be prepared to stop or ask if you may pass. When approaching equestrians, it is especially important that you do not spook the horses. They are much bigger than you and can be easily be startled. If you see equestrians ahead, stop on the side of the trail and let them pass. If you are traveling in the same direction, maintain the same speed as the horses, but keep your distance and ask the rider if it is alright to pass. If so, all bikers should pass on the same side of the horse to avoid confusing the animal.

Hydration and nutrition

Your body is like an engine. It requires fuel, conditioning, fine tuning, and maintenance. Two factors which directly affect your body's performance are hydration and nutrition. Dehydration is caused by the loss of body fluids without adequate rehydration. Heat and intensity of the ride contributes to the dehydration process. Choose the cooler hours of the day when attempting long or steep uphill rides. Listen to your body and know when to rest and cool down. Just fifteen minutes of riding can raise your core temperature by five degrees fahrenheit.

Adequate hydration will dramatically decrease your chances of heat illness and fatigue. Fluids help increase blood volume and aid in transport of oxygen, nutrients and waste products in your circulatory system. Your natural ability to cool down by sweat evaporation depends on excess fluid volume. So, drink plenty of water and electrolyte replacements before, during and after your ride. Keep in mind that solutions which yield high levels of sugars or salts may cause stomach upset and diarrhea. Each person may react differently to these products.

Drinking plenty of water the day before is a good tip for all riders, regardless of condition and weight. During your workout, try to consume six to eight ounces of fluid every 15 minutes. This would exceed the contents of the average water bottle in just one hour. Camelbak Hydration Systems® offer up to 100 ounces of fluid capacity which is convenient to carry on your back. The durable Camelbak also has multiple designs to carry other essentials such as nutrition bars, pump and your biking guide.

Nutrition is equally important for performance and endurance. Eating right can make a world of difference in your overall performance. High carbohydrate meals such as spaghetti, breads and pasta can help. Bananas are a great source of potassium. This helps

breakdown lactic acid your muscles produce during heavy exercise. But, once you begin that long grueling uphill, it's hardly appropriate to carry a bunch of bananas and a bowl of pasta. A number of tasty nutrition bars are on the market. PowerBar®, supporters of athletes world wide, offers a variety of flavors that are sure to satisfy your taste buds. When you feel the need for that extra boost of energy, indulge in a snack worth snackin', eat a PowerBar. PowerGel®, a nutrition gel, is also available and aids in faster digestion. Your body processes the nutrition it needs from a gel instead of having to breakdown a solid food.

Before you ride

Use the following check list to ensure a successful ride. It may seem like a lot of preparation, but it should be standard practice.

- At least one hour before you ride, eat a good meal. Plenty of carbohydrates the night before will help get you over the hill and back again.
- Stretching is a great warm-up and helps to prevent muscle injury.
- Bring your helmet, shoes, gloves, shades, sunscreen, full water supply, and foul weather gear (as needed).
- Hydrate yourself with plenty of water at least an hour before your ride. Carry more water than you think you'll need.
- Carry a small tool bag which includes pump, tire patch kit, chain breaker, allen wrench set with flathead and phillips screwdrivers attached, 10mm wrench and tire pries.
- Additional equipment may include an extra tire tube, a light for night riders, snacks for the long rides, a first aid kit (bee sting kit or medications as needed) and a cellular phone for emergencies.
- Check your tire pressure (suggested p.s.i. is labeled on tire), shock pressure and adjustable settings, and tighten any loose hardware.
  Now, you are ready for the trail. Have fun!

Theft

As with any valuable item, you should always take precautions to protect your bike. We have thieves here in Hawai'i, just like anywhere else. Mountain bikes are hot commodities for thieves. It is a good idea not to rely on a bicycle lock for protection. If you really want to protect your bike from thieves, don't ever lock it, meaning, don't ever leave it unattended. Even the most expensive locks can be easily broken. One minute is all it takes, so play it safe and keep your bike with you at all times.

When you park a car at a trail head, be sure to obey parking signs. Keep your vehicle locked and don't leave any valuables in the car. A lot of broken glass on the ground may indicate a high crime area, so park somewhere else, perhaps in a residential area. After all, you have a bike, so make use of it and keep your vehicle safe.

Bicycle Maintenance
Back to the basics

Your mountain bike should be well maintained and lubricated at all times. Components that are well kept will give you much more accurate responses and last longer. Schedule regular maintenance for your bike. Owning your own tools and knowing how to use them should help to minimize the overhaul and repair costs.

It would serve you well to know how to fix a flat. This is a basic skill that requires no technical expertise. Many of Hawai'i's low land dry forests have an abundance of kiawe trees. The thorns from the kiawe tree are often strewn across the trail and can cause multiple punctures in your tires.

First, consider preventing a flat. You may insert a tire liner that fits between your tube and tire. Made of durable puncture-proof plastic, tire liners help to deflect most small thorns and sharp objects.

Another product available is a gooey substance that coats the inside of your tube. When a small puncture occurs, this goo leaks out and quickly dries, temporarily sealing the leak.

These are not guarantees, merely prevention. It is to your advantage to be able to fix your own flat when out on a trail. If you haven't already, learn to remove and replace both tire and tube. If nothing more than a small hole, five minutes and a five cent rubber patch will get you back up and riding.

Check all bolts and connections before and after each ride and tighten any loose hardware as needed. Inspect and re-pack the bearings in your headset, bottom bracket and hubs at least once a year. Do this more often if you are riding regularly in wet and muddy conditions.

Bearing grease such as Bullshot® and Finish Line® are formulated specifically for bicycle use. Some riders use a more water resilient grease designed for boat trailers but, it is more viscous and tends to create unneeded drag.

The headset takes a lot of abuse and can sometimes become loose. To check it, lock the front brake by pulling the lever tight. Roll the bike forward and backward to feel for play in the headset. If you feel play, tighten the headset immediately.

Wheel hubs can be checked by holding the bike firmly and moving the rim laterally. Use the same check for the bottom bracket. Grab the crank arm and move it laterally to check for play.

Brake and shifting cables should be greased within the cable housing when possible. Worn, rusty or frayed cables are dangerous and can snap at critical moments. Don't wait. If these inexpensive items are worn, replace them.

Chains take a lot of stress and should be inspected often for rust and deformities. Chains can be checked with a special tool that is made to measure the amount of stretch in the chain. This will help to determine replacement needs. Lubricate the chain as often as possible and especially after wet and muddy rides. Use a good Teflon lubricant like Tri-Flow® for your chain and derailleurs.

Correct derailleur adjustment provides smooth and accurate shifting. If your derailleur doesn't line up with cogs or sprockets, an obvious grinding or clicking noise will remind you that an adjustment is needed.

Inspect your brake

pads to be sure that they are set properly. Otherwise, you will hear an obnoxious squeal known as the "mountain bike mating call". Improper adjustment can also lead to brake failure or sudden tire wall blow out.

If you have a suspension package on your bike, check under the boots for any leaky cylinders and clean out dust and debris. Inspect the crown and mount for stress cracks and loose bolts. The suspension absorbs shock and impact and deserves routine inspection. Suspension products should only be serviced by an authorized service center.

Even with the high-tech engineering of today's frames, stress cracks and broken frames are still a part of life. Riding styles which include jumping, drop-offs, hard crashes and collisions can lead to frame damage. Stressed areas can be found during routine cleaning.

Check your tires for worn side walls, ballooning and imbedded objects. A high speed blow out is not something you want to experience.

Lift the bike and free spin the wheels to check for rim deformities. Out-of-round or cracked rims should be replaced and out-of-true rims should be repaired. Bent, loose or broken spokes can weaken a rim's integrity. Replace any bad spokes.

If you do not have the time or the patience to be a grease monkey, take your bike to the professionals for service. With a routine maintenance program, you'll enjoy more time on the trail than off it.

Cleaning your bike

Keeping your mountain bike clean and well lubricated will enhance the life of your paint, components and accessories. Simple Green®, diluted with water, makes an excellent cleaning solution. Use a wet sponge or cloth to apply soap to the bike, then rinse thoroughly with water. Avoid spraying concentrated soap directly onto bike.

On shoreline trails, your bike will be subjected to a high level of salt spray, so wash it the same day you rode it. Sand is gritty and washes off quite easily. If you leave the sand on your bike, it will add wear on brakes, rims, chain and sprockets, so clean as often as possible.

Much of our island soil consists of red dirt. The fine powder from red dirt gets into everything and riding on these roads with light colored clothing can permanently stain your clothes. On dry days, these roads are a lot of fun to ride on. However, if it rains, your ride may soon be over. In some areas, the dirt turns into a clay-like mud. This stuff sticks to your tires, spokes, chain, brakes and shoes. You will end up walking your bike, your footwear will resemble platform shoes and your tires, well, good luck. Most of the time, 15 to 25 feet is the maximum distance your tires will roll before you have to scrape the mud off. When it gets bad, hopefully you won't be too far from a paved road or civilization.

Cleaning your bike after riding it in clay-like mud is a major chore. It is best to wait a day and let the mud dry. Then break off the dried chunks, add them to your garden, and proceed with routine cleaning. Don't forget your chain, derailleurs and cables should always be lubricated after every cleaning to ensure that they operate smoothly.

Hawai'i's Competition Scene
The good, the bad and the muddy

Since the early 1980's, the number of Hawai'i's mountain bike competitors has grown threefold. Smaller races are held between riders and friends, however, larger more organized events, with support from the National Off-Road Mountain Biking Association (NORBA), have brought Hawai'i's competition scene to an all new high.

On the island of O'ahu, racing events at Bellows, Kahuku, and Helemano have almost become a thing of the past, while Ka'a'awa Valley at Kualoa Ranch became the new hot spot for local and international competitions on both the professional and amateur circuit.

The largest of competitions at Ka'a'awa was the Outrigger Hotels of Hawai'i Hawaiian Mountain Tour Pro/Am, put on by TEAM UNLIMITED from 1995-1997. Professional mountain bikers from around the globe came to Hawai'i to battle it out, including all time world champions John Tomac, Thomas Frischknecht, Tinker Juarez, Miguel Martinez, Dave Weins, Missy Giove, Alison Sydor, Leigh Donovan, and many others.

Alison Sydor, XC winner of the 1997 Hawaiian Mountain Tour.
photo: Twain Newhart

With the valley's location on the northeastern side of O'ahu, the weather holds many surprises. During one event, rain showers turned the course to mud and created less than desirable conditions. At the jump, some riders toughed it out choosing slower, safer paths while other brave dogs showed off their stuff with a "NO FEAR" attitude and plenty of high flying aerial maneuvers.

Many racers believe that, one of the most challenging elements for mountain bike racing in Hawai'i is overcoming the tropical heat and humidity. But, that doesn't slow them down.

Top competitors who have traveled to numerous racing events around the world agreed that Hawai'i has some of the most incredible landscape and year-round riding conditions. The majestic volcanic mountains of this island paradise make Hawai'i highly desirable for many more international events.

Another such event was the Grundig/UCI World Cup of Mountain Biking Finals. Held on O'ahu in September 1996, this global event hosted 325 professional mountain bikers from 23 different countries. The downhill event was held at Wa'ahila Ridge on O'ahu's south shore. Starting from deep in a Norfolk pine forest of St. Louis Heights, this 1.6 mile downhill course was changed forever when it received international television coverage and fame. The

Bill Barnfield riding to victory!
stock photo

course was wet and muddy at the top and challenged riders with its slick surface and steep drop-off section which widened the eyes of every competitor. Meanwhile, at the bottom of the course, a menagerie of riders with their hitech mountain bikes held spectators in awe. The newer downhill bikes, with a plush six inches of suspension travel front and rear, gave those riders an edge over their competitors who were riding cross-country bikes with only half the travel.

In recent years, mountain biking slid its way into other aspects of competitive racing. During 1995 on O'ahu, TEAM BOCA organized Hawai'i's first off-road triathlon. The Mountain Man Triathlon attracted a mixture of athletes who competed in a rough water swim, mountain bike course and trail run through the pristine Ka'a'awa Valley at Kualoa Ranch.

Waimea Valley on O'ahu's north shore was once home to Hawai'i Mountain Bike Adventures who operated the state's first official downhill course. A landslide ceased its operations in early 2000. Today, Waimea Valley hosts off-road competitions including the popular Mountain Man Triathlon, Eco-Challenge and occasional mountain bike races.

Since 1996, the Aquaterra incorporated mountain biking into its

Joey Riveira flying at the Hawaiian Mountain Tour. photo: Twain Newhart

off-road triathlons on Maui. Produced by TEAM UNLIMITED, the now Xterra attracts famous triathletes such as Scott Tinley, Mike Pigg, Jimmy Riccitello and mountain bike professionals such as Ned Overend and Shari Kain. Up and coming local cyclist, Allegra Erisman won the 2000 World Championship in the 15-19 year old class.

Also on Maui, Ehman Productions held the Maui Ultimate Challenge on Haleakala in 1995. This exhilarating invitational event combined a paved uphill race and an off-road downhill race. The uphill race offered a physically demanding course, going

from sea level to the summit of the 10,023 foot volcano. O'ahu's Ray Brust, won the uphill in only 3 hours 7 minutes and also won first overall.

On Kaua'i, the Powerline Outlaw Race has been an annual event since 1987. John Sargeant, Todd Melton, Jason Irons and Jed Smith are among the top riders who aren't newcomers to the rugged and challenging Powerline Trail.

Hawai'i's list of up-and-coming riders continues to grow. Long time competitors such as O'ahu's Bill Barnfield, Chris Clark, Ray Brust, Alaska Dambacher, John Blanck and Josh Overton, and Big Islands Garuda McCarthy and Chris

Alaska Dambacher - Oakley pro rider
photo: Twain Newhart

Seymour continue to dominate the expert division in island-wide racing.

In 2000, local Master, Bill Barnfield competed for the "US Team" at the World Championships in Bromont, Quebec, Canada and at the US National Championships at Mammoth, CA. At the Worlds, Bill took 1st Place in the Downhill, Masters 50-54 years old class. That made Bill the 2000 World Champion in his class.

In 2002, Scott Chaney and The Bike Shop conducted the first "24 Hours of Hell in Paradise". This 24 hour non-stop mountain bike race was held at Ka'a'awa Valley, O'ahu. With its island wide attention, we should be seeing this as an annual event.

O'ahu's Alaska Dambacher (Raging Isle) and Joey Riveira (Bikefactory) have accelerated through the ranks and have also taken their talents to the mainland to compete in the NORBA Nationals. After successfully finishing in the top five overall placing, both Alaska and Joey were upgraded to professional status and now hold a NORBA PRO racing license. These local riders have permanently engraved their names into the list of the good, the bad and the muddy. For updated race info, visit www.bikehawaii.com

7 Traveling Inter-Island
Easy ways to island hop

Planning your Hawaiian mountain bike vacation can be a simple procedure if you make the right connections.

Congratulations! Having this book in your possession is your first step to a successful adventure. It is important that you arrange your transportation and accommodations in advance to avoid getting stuck between a rock and a hard place. If you are lucky, you might have a friend or a relative that can put you up during your travels. However, if you don't have a local connection, here are some great travel tips.

Mountain bike rentals are not so bad these days. You can pretty much count on being able to rent suspension bikes and decent gear from the various bike

shops on each island. Check the Appendix for a list of bike shops.

Admittedly, there is no substitution for the feel of your own bike between your legs. With that in mind, the following information may help answer the many travelling questions that you might have.

First, if your visiting from out-of-state, getting your mountain bike to Hawai'i is perhaps the most vulnerable part of your journey. Larger aircraft carry larger quantities of luggage and, therefore, you should take extra precautions to protect your bike from potential damage. Hard shell bike cases can be purchased to allow for maximum protection. However, simple cardboard bike boxes make for relatively safe and inexpensive bike travel. If you are a member of the International Mountain Bicycling Association (IMBA), your bike can travel free from the U.S. mainland to Honolulu and back. Riders should contact IMBA for further information. International travelers can substitute one piece of luggage for a boxed bike and also have it travel free.

When flying inter-island, most airlines do not require you to box your bike. While each airline does have individual requirements, the safest means of travel for your bike is to pack it in a protective hard shell case. However, for many, this is not convenient and not always practical, since you will need to carry the case around with you after you land.

Most airlines have a damage waiver of liability which limits their liability to $1,250. If your bike exceeds this value, additional insurance may be purchased from the airline, to a maximum value of $2,500. Some credit card companies offer full value protection for travelers and there luggage, so check with your credit card company for details.

Here in Hawai'i, one airline tries hard to accommodate the traveling cyclist. Aloha Airlines flies Boeing 737's, and their sister company, Island Air, utilizes twin turbo props. Between the two airlines, you can fly to any of the six major islands.

Aloha Airlines offers convenience and flexibility. You can literally mountain bike down from a lush rain forest, across town and straight to the ticket counter. However, muddy bicycles are discouraged, so clean it as necessary. Aloha Airlines makes it easy by allowing for mountain bikes to be wheeled up to the ticket counter and checked in as special baggage.

They do require you to remove your pedals to prevent scratching other people's luggage and loosen the stem/handle bars and turn them sideways to allow for more space. Be prepared and carry your pedal and allen wrench. Remove any loose items that could fall off during transport. For example, remove your water bottle, cyclometer, and any clip on pumps or lights. Keep in mind that bicycles traveling with you require a small fee and may be subject to space availability.

For alternatives to air travel, an inter-island ferry service is available between the islands of Maui and Lana'i. The Expeditions "Lana'i Ferry" will transport you and your bike from the old whaling port of Lahaina, Maui and set out for a forty-five

minute cruise across the 'Au'au Channel to Manele Harbor, Lana'i. If you're lucky, you might even catch a glimpse of dolphins or humpback whales during your journey across.

However you get to the next island, be sure to have your rent-a-car confirmation number, driver's license and credit card ready. Dollar Rent-A-Car are long-time supporters of mountain biking events here in the islands. Dollar Rent-A-Car has transportation available on all six of the Hawaiian Islands. They provide a wide selection of reliable automobiles and four-wheel drives at reasonable rates.

For accommodations, you'll be sure to receive plenty of Hawaiian hospitality at Outrigger Hotels of Hawai'i. With comfortable hotels and condos on O'ahu, Maui, Kaua'i and Hawai'i, Outrigger Hotels' reputation is second to none. Outrigger Hotels are also long-time supporters of professional mountain biking competitions here in Hawai'i. Outrigger has provided the best for the best, such as Missy Giove, John Tomac, Tomas Misser, David Weins, Miguel Martinez and Thomas Frischknecht, just to name a few.

Camping is also a popular and economical way to visit Hawai'i. If camping interests you, check the Appendix and call the appropriate agency about permits and availability. Contact numbers for travel accommodations are also in the Appendix.

photo: NASA

*The Hawaiian Islands from a different perspective. From bottom right to top;
Niʻihau, Kauaʻi, Oʻahu, Molokaʻi, Lanaʻi, Maui, Kahoʻolawe and Hawaiʻi.
photo: NASA*

MAP LEGEND

ICONS:

 FOREST

 VIEW POINT

 PARKING

 950' ELEVATION

 12.6 DISTANCE IN MILES

 AIRPORT

 TELEPHONE

 STRUCTURES

CLIFF HAZARD

STEEP/DROP OFF

DISMOUNT

FOOT PATH ONLY

RESTROOMS

CAMPING

PICNIC AREA

HIGHWAY #

DIFFICULTY RATINGS:

♦♦♦ ADVANCED

♦♦ INTERMEDIATE

♦ BEGINNER

TRAILS & ROADS:

——————
SINGLE TRACK

- - - - - - - - -
FOOT PATH ONLY

━━━━━━
PAVED ROAD

▪▪▪▪▪▪▪▪▪▪
4WD ROAD

▬▬▬▬▬▬
PUBLIC HWY OR ROAD

LOCATION MAP:

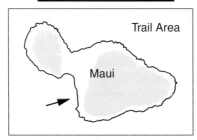

ARROW POINTS TO LOCATION OF TRAIL

Hawai'i - The Big Island

The Hawaiian Islands are one of the most isolated groups of islands in the world. They are over 2,000 miles from the nearest continental land mass. For this reason, rare species of tropical birds, plants and animals that exist no where else in the world have evolved here. These exotic species are sometimes seen in the dense rainforests. With active volcanoes, earthquakes, and bizarre weather patterns, the island of Hawai'i makes for mystical and exciting mountain biking adventures that are almost prehistoric.

As the largest of the Hawaiian Islands, the "Big Island" of Hawai'i lives up to its popular nickname. Hawai'i is 4,038 square miles of some of the most diverse tropical environment on earth. It is 93 miles long, 76 miles wide and is home to the tallest mountain in the world, the southern-most point in the United States, and one of the most active volcanoes on the planet.

Without a doubt, the Big Island of Hawai'i will be one of your most enjoyable experiences of mountain biking on earth. Have fun and don't forget your camera.

Mauna Kea

The island is made up of five volcanic mountains. The two largest are Mauna Kea and Mauna Loa. The other three are Kohala, Hualalai and Kilauea. Mauna Kea is the highest peak in the state standing at 13,796 feet and is covered with snow for about three months out of the year. Measured from its base on the ocean floor, Mauna Kea is the tallest mountain in the world standing near 32,000 feet, even taller than Mt. Everest. During the winter months, Mauna Kea becomes a playground for local skiers, snowboarders, bodyboarders and even mountain bikers. While there are no biking trails near the summit, extreme cyclists still enjoy the thrill and challenge of the road climb up and, of course, the "bombing" downhill along the steep gravel and paved road.

Caution is advised to Mauna Kea riders. Certain health risks may be associated with high elevations. Oxygen deficiency at high altitudes can cause headaches, dizziness and nausea. Riders should be in good health and acclimate at the Onizuka Center for International Astronomy (OCIA) Visitors Center at the 9,300 foot level, before proceeding to the summit. Gas, food and other provisions are not available on Mauna Kea. Prepare for high winds, rain, sleet and snow with temperatures well below freezing, even during summer months. 4WD vehicles are recommended above the OCIA Visitors Information Center. Before attempting Mauna Kea summit, call for updated weather information at 969-3218 or the visitor information line at 961-2180.

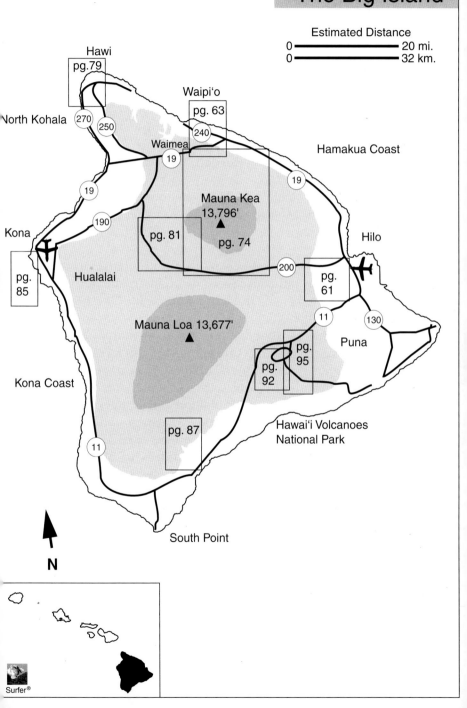

Kulani Forest

How to get there: Located just south of Hilo. Head towards Hawai'i Volcanoes National Park on Highway 11. Between the 4 and 5 mile markers, turn right onto Stainback Highway or W. Mamaki and proceed for approximately 2.5 miles. The access road into the forest will be on your left. Parking is available outside the forest or near the quarry, just .4 mile in.

Kulani Forest: Various distances
Rating: Beginner to advanced
Special: State land. No permit needed. Forest slated for harvest in near future.
Note: Dirt roads and single track. Use caution when wet.
Hazards: Occasional motorcycles and 4WD's. Slippery roots and rocks when wet.
Amenities: None.
History: Since the 1960's, reforestation of eucalyptus, Queensland maple and Australian red cedar were made in an attempt to establish locally grown timber for furniture. *Kulani*, lit. "like heaven".
Elevation Range: 500 to 800+ feet

Kulani Forest has an abundance of single track trails that weave in and out of fern ground cover and tall timberland forest. This sloping sectional piece of land offers riders a choice of mild grade access roads or technical single track. The roads encompass the entire forest and compliment the multiple single track by offering riders an easy return to the starting position. Each trail is unique in its own way and varies in difficulty. Sometimes used for local mountain bike racing, Kulani is a must for riders of all skill levels. Beginner riders may want to stay on the access roads for easy maneuvering, while intermediate and advanced riders may share the challenging single track. Riders should be prepared for wet conditions as rain is common here on the lower slopes of Mauna Loa. The porous volcanic cinder quickly absorbs standing water, leaving trail surfaces with minimal puddling.

Trail nicknames such as, "Lower and Upper Criterium", "Long and Grassy", "Never Never Land", "Frustration Trail" and "Boulder Dash" are just a few of the descriptions to match the terrain. If you're planning a mountain biking trip on the Big Island, don't miss Kulani Forest. You'll never forget it. It is literally, "like heaven".

Kulani Forest

Trails

◆ Beginner

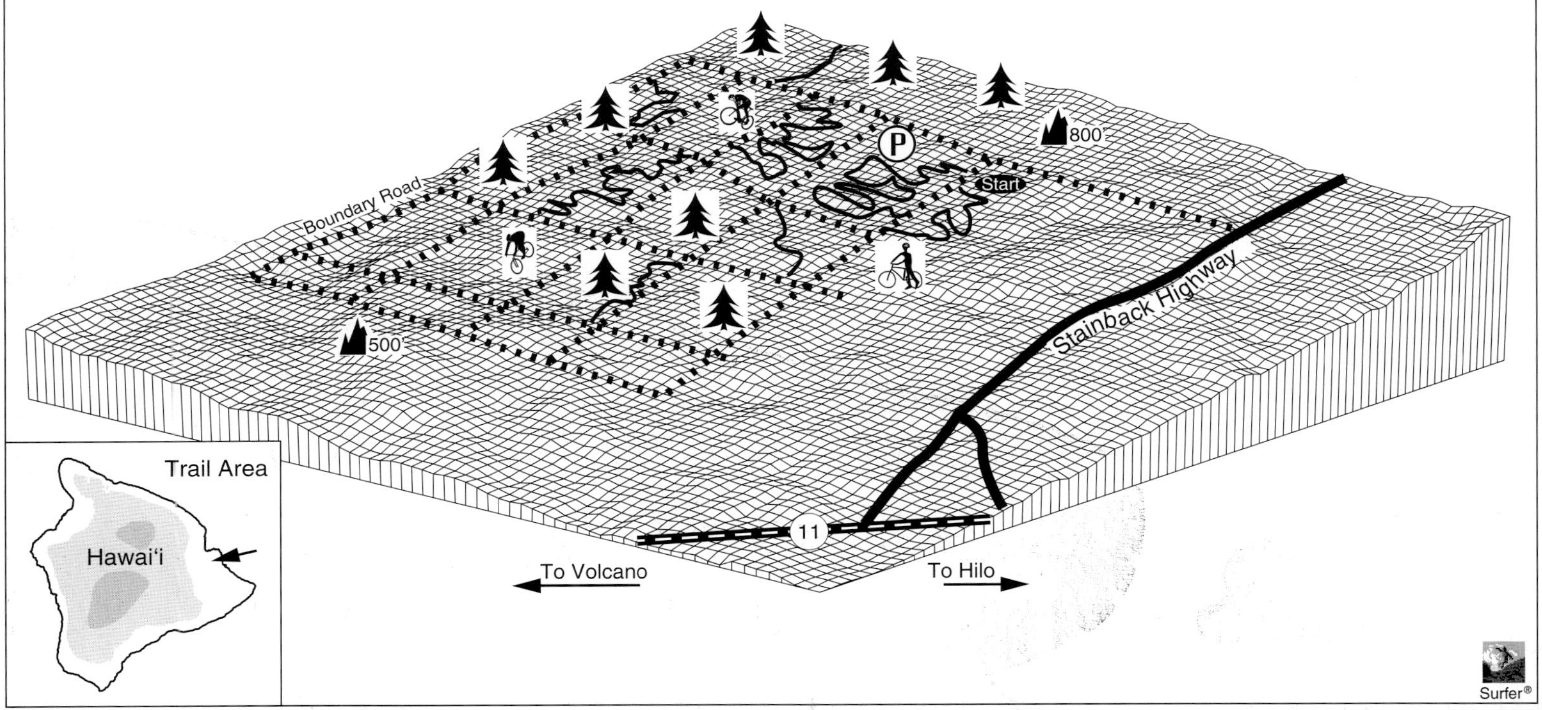

Stainback Highway

800

Start

P

Boundary Road

500

To Hilo

11

To Volcano

Trail Area

Hawai'i

Surfer®

Mud Lane

How to get there: From Waimea, head east towards Waipi'o on Mamalahoa Highway 19. Access is located approximately 100 yards before the 52 mile marker. Park just off the highway at the junction of Old Mamalahoa Highway and Highway 19. Access to Mud Lane is down the 1.7 mile paved and gravel road directly across from the junction, just left of the golf course.

Mud Lane: Approximately 5.2 miles one way
Rating: Beginner to intermediate
Special: No permits needed
Note: 4WD road.
Hazards: Loose rocks and gravel, ruts, possible recreational vehicles. Muddy when wet.
Amenities: None
History: Built in the early 1800's, this road was the old stagecoach highway from Honoka'a to Waimea. Later, it was used as an access road for Hamakua Sugar which closed its operations in October 1994.
Elevation Range: 2,800 to 700 feet

This gravel and dirt road begins from the Mamalahoa Highway 19 and descends 1.7 miles through groves of eucalyptus and kahili ginger ending at a guava and ironwood forest. Proceed straight into the forest to find .4 mile of fun and challenging serpentine single track strewn with roots and obstacles. At the 2.1 mile mark, the trail forks. Go left to access Mud Lane. (Going right would take you to Grubbies Trail. See map)

Once you reach the dirt road, go right and continue down. This area is often fragrant with the smell of fresh yellow ginger that flourishes here. You will need to dismount to get over some of the fallen trees that lay across the road. After carefully negotiating the rugged road, use caution as you begin to pick up the pace. Conditions on this unimproved road change often due to the heavy rain and run off, which also give the road its popular name, Mud Lane. Some wild sugar cane still grows in this area, remnants of the former Hamakua plantation. Great ocean views are also found along this rugged downhill.

Since the closure of Hamakua Sugar in 1994, Mud Lane has since become eroded and overgrown with bushes and shrubs, as well as littered with fallen trees and branches. It can be accessed

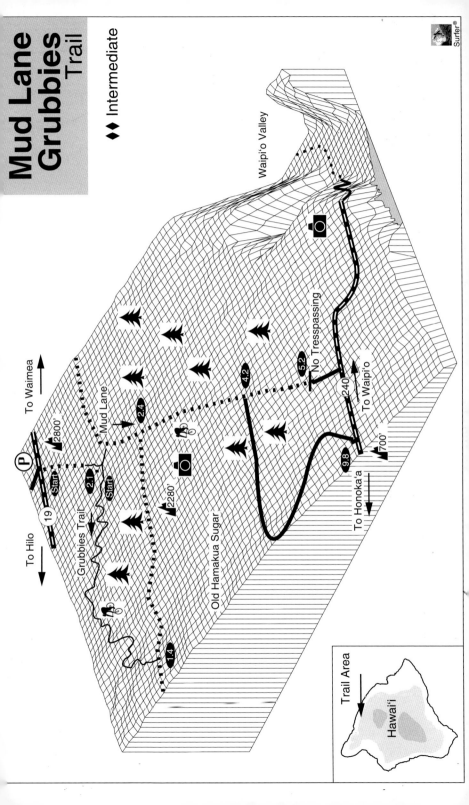

first as a downhill, then you'll need to pedal back up this hot and rugged uphill. Some riders prefer to ride the uphill first and downhill last.

At 4.2 miles, you can turn right and follow a paved road 5.6 miles to exit onto Highway 240 (see map) or continue down another mile to a gate with a no trespassing sign. Turn around here and proceed back up, or follow the paved road out to Highway 240. Turn left onto Highway 240 and ride for approximately 6 miles to catch an unforgettable view of historic Waipi'o Valley, which used to be home to hundreds of native Hawaiians who farmed taro as a way of life. Enjoy the ride back up!

Crater Rim Trail, Hawai'i Volcanoes National Park

Snow covered pu'u on Mauna Kea.

High above the clouds with Haleakala, Maui seen in the distance, Skyline.

Grubbies Trail with Hapu'u tree fern.

Steam vents, HI. Volcanoes Ntl. Park

The ten mile downhill from Skyline offers numerous jumps for those who dare.

The timberlands of Kulani Forest.

During the snowy winter months, locals make the most of Mauna Kea's summit.

Rustic accommodations are perfect for multi-day mountain bike tours.

HI. Volcanoes Ntl. Park. photo: NPS

Night riding at Pine Trees.

The green pastures of Pu'uhue Road.

Rainbow Falls

Riding high in the clouds, Mauna Kea.

A great way to commute between trails   Escape Road, HI. Volcanoes Ntl. Park

View toward Hilo from Mana Road.

A rider gazes out over the sleeping Kilauea Caldera and Halemaʻumaʻu Crater.

Grassy slopes of Mauna Kea, Parker Ranch.

Grubbies Trail

How to get there: Follow the directions for Mud Lane.
Grubbies Trail: 1.4 miles one way
Rating: Intermediate to advanced
Special: Property of Hamakua Sugar. Contact 776-1244 for further info. Suggest riding Mud Lane first to become familiar with area.
Note: Single track. Do not ride when wet.
Hazards: Roots, rocks, steep sections and occasional motorcycles.
Amenities: None
History: The single track within this area is cut and kept open by motorcycles.
Elevation Range: 2,800 to 2,280 feet

Following the directions for Mud Lane, turn right at the fork when you reach 2.1 miles in. (Going left will take you to Mud Lane. See map) On your immediate right are the remains of an old outdoor bread oven that was built next to a plantation cottage in the 1920's.

Grubbies Trail (aka: Priscilla's Trail) is 1.4 miles of challenging single track, but round trip from Highway 19 is approximately 7.2 miles. After the fast downhill from the highway over the gravel road, get ready for some wild, single trackin' fun! This technical single track is strewn with roots, rocks and has a variety of short and steep hill climbs and drop-offs. Surrounded by hapu'u tree ferns and guava trees, you will encounter an occasional fallen eucalyptus tree that will require riders to dismount.

At approximately 3.5 miles in, the single track ends and you will intersect with an old dirt road. Go left and follow the overgrown road for one mile before intersecting with Mud Lane. Go left again and ride up .6 mile and turn left back onto the single track. This is where the old bread oven is. From here, it's a 2.1 mile pedal back up to the Highway 19. If you still have the energy, ride Mud Lane down and back, or repeat Grubbies Trail once, twice or three times more.

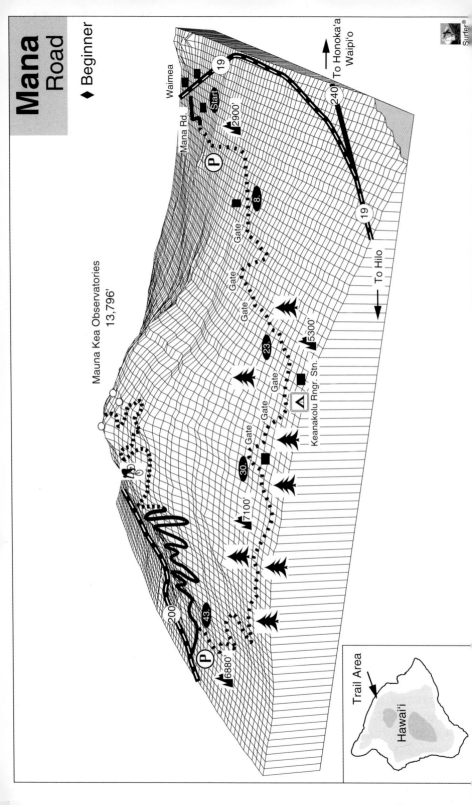

Mana Road

How to get there: From Waimea, head east towards Waipi'o on Mamalahoa Highway 19. Mana Road will be on your right across from the 55 mile marker.

Mana Road can also be accessed from the south-facing side of Mauna Kea. Head up the Saddle Road, turn up John A. Burns Way at the 28 mile marker. Road name signs may not be present. Continue up Mauna Kea for 2 miles and turn right onto the dirt road. This is the preferred entrance to Mana Road, if you plan on riding the entire distance. Have someone drop you off and pick you up later in Waimea at a specified time.

Mana Road: 43 miles one way
Rating: Beginner to advanced
Special: Public road which is maintained by Hawai'i County. Cuts through private property of Parker Ranch, Department of Hawaiian Home Lands (DHHL) and other ranch land. No permit needed. Close all gates behind you. Stay on main road, and don't spook the livestock.
Note: Dirt road.
Hazards: Recreational vehicles. Livestock. Rapid weather changes. Possible hypothermal conditions. Prepare for freezing temperatures, winds, and rain.
Amenities: None
History: Part of this road was used as a shortcut to Hilo in the 1800's. *Mana,* lit. "arid" or "supernatural power".
Parker Ranch property. Call 885-7311 for the visitors center.
Elevation Range: 2,900 to 7,100 feet

This dirt road stretches 43 miles across the base of Mauna Kea from its southeastern face around to its northern face. Starting from either side, Mana Road can be ridden as a scenic out and back with plenty of challenging uphill climbs and fast downhills.

Starting from Waimea, Mana Road is a mild uphill beginning at 2,900 feet. This is the preferred access for beginners as a partial out and back. It begins with 1.2 miles of paved road from Mamalahoa Highway 19, gradually ascends Mauna Kea's northern base and wraps around to the east. This area is often foggy, misty and some times rainy, so be prepared for cold, moist conditions. A long sleeve, water-resistant jacket and even long riding pants will keep you drier and warmer if it rains. Some spectacular views are found along the rolling pasture lands. The North Kohala mountains, as well as the summit observatories on Mauna Kea are visible with clear skies.

If you intend to ride the entire length, start from the southeastern side just off the Saddle Road. This route begins at the 6,880 foot level and provides fantastic cross country riding with a variety of up and downhill grades. Bring a camera to capture the awesome rainbows mixed within the clouds, and various light shows and shadows from the tropical sun that penetrate the misty cloud layers. Ride as little or as long as you would like and enjoy the ride. It is a long 43 mile ride to Waimea, so allow a minimum of 4 to 6 hours for strong riders. Recreational riders will still enjoy the scenic beauty as a partial out and back if desired.

Pu'uhue Road

How to get there: Mauka access: On North Kohala's Highway 250 between the 17 and 18 mile marker. At the entrance to this paved road, you will see a small sign marked Pu'uhue. Turn down and follow for .75 mile. Enter the grassy pasture road on right just past the cattle guard. Proceed through the gate.

Makai access: Heading towards Hawi on Highway 270, turn right uphill just before the 18 mile marker. From here, it is 5 miles to the ranch.

Pu'uhue Road: 10 miles round trip
Rating: Beginner to intermediate
Special: No permit needed.
Note: Dirt road through private pastures. Stay on main road.
Hazards: Vehicles, horses and livestock.
Amenities: None
History: Old government ranch road. *Pu'u* lit. "peak". *Hue* lit. "gourd or narrow necked vessel to hold water".
Elevation Range: 2,000 to 450 feet

Pu'uhue Road is a great ride for the mountain biker that wants to get a workout without all the fancy footwork of narrow single track. Connecting the coastal Highway 270 with the upper Highway 250, Pu'uhue Road is a scenic ride with beautiful green pasture lands of the Kohala Coast that contrast with the deep blue Pacific Ocean. Vistas of the neighboring island of Maui make for an unforgettable off-road experience.

Be sure to stay on the main road as you will be surrounded by private pastures with livestock and working ranches.

The downhill is twice the fun in the sun. With many open lines of sight, riders can easily view the road ahead for obstacles and/or other enthusiasts. Pu'uhue Road is highly recommended for the beginner biker that wants off-road experience with some physical challenges. Don't forget your camera.

'Upolu Point

How to get there: From Waimea, Hawi is approximately 22 miles north on Highway 250. At the junction of Highway 270, turn left and pass Hawi town and turn right towards the ocean at the 20 mile marker or the 'Upolu Airport sign. The two mile, bumpy, paved road will take you down 700 feet to sea level to 'Upolu Airport, a short landing strip for small aircraft. Park here and follow the dirt road to the right along the fence line.

'Upolu Point: Approximately 6 miles round trip
Rating: Beginner to advanced
Special: No permit needed on dirt road. For access beyond the gate marked "private property", contact Chalon International 889-6257
Note: Dirt road
Hazards: Vehicular traffic, sea cliffs and loose terrain
Amenities: None
History: Kamehameha 'akahi Aina Hanau, and Mo'okini Heiau, built in 480 A.D.
Elevation Range: 100 feet

'Upolu Point offers visitors a special treat to the Big Island of Hawai'i. Besides fun terrain for mountain biking, several important ancient historical sites are found along this pristine coastline.

Follow the dirt road east along the airport fence line. The trail will loop back around on the makai side of the airstrip and head west. Great views of Maui across the 'Alenuihaha Channel are found along the entire point. The trail will lead you to two historic landmarks which are testimonials to the hard and enduring work of the ancient Hawaiians. The first is Mo'okini Heiau, a sacred place of worship dated back to 480 A.D. The second is the birthplace of King Kamehameha I.

This is a hot, dry area and riders should be prepared. At the 3 mile mark, the dirt road ends at a gated entrance to an old government housing area. This is the turn around point. From here, turn around and head back along the same coastal path. Because of the rocky shoreline in this area, swimming is not recommended.

'Upolu Point
Pu'uhue Road

◆ Beginner

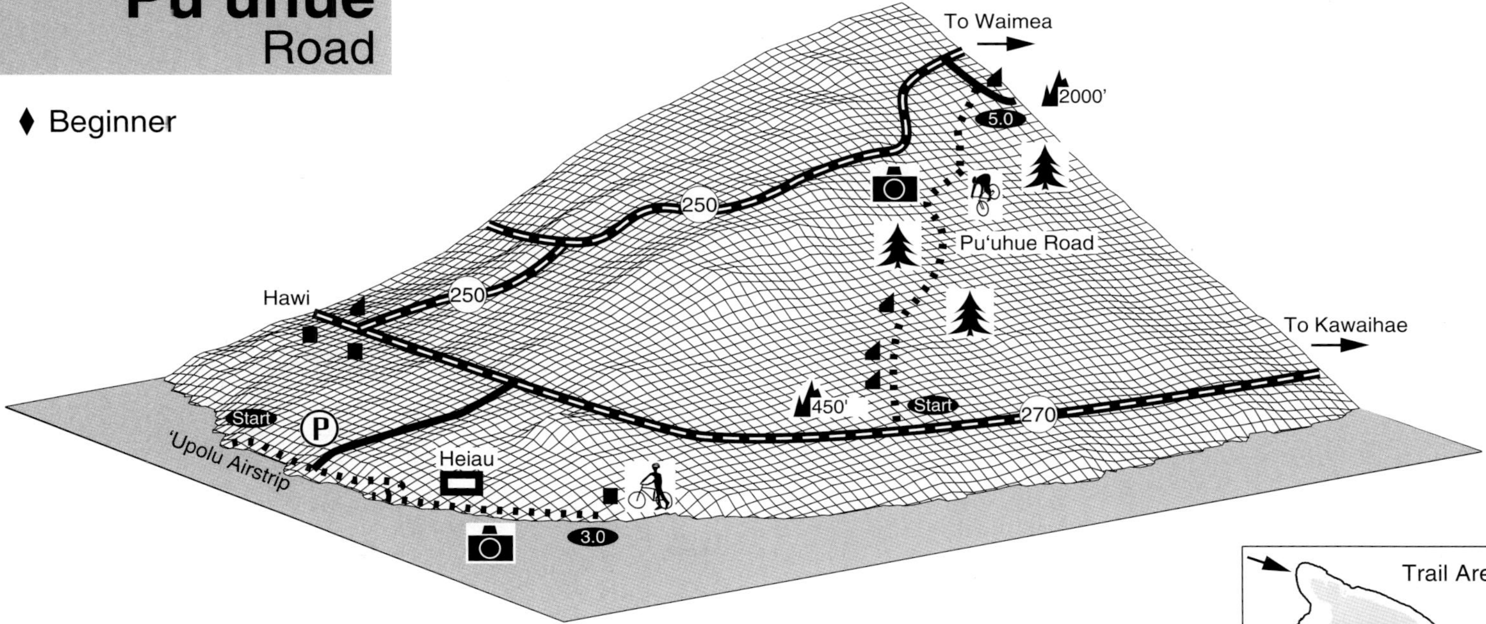

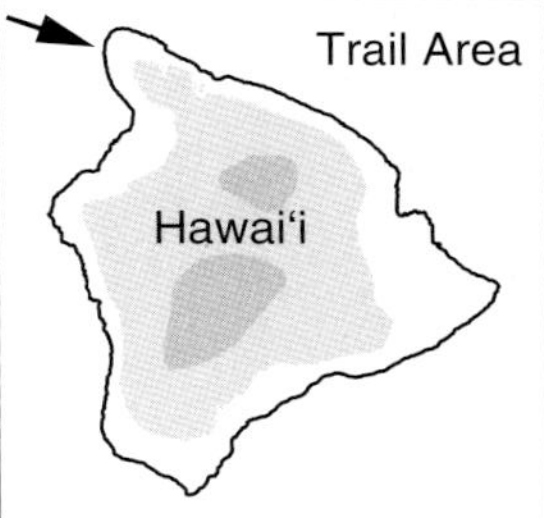

Trail Area

Hawai'i

To Kawaihae

To Waimea

2000'

5.0

Pu'uhue Road

270

Start

450

250

250

3.0

Hawi

Heiau

Start

P

'Upolu Airstrip

Surfer®

Skyline Trail

How to get there: Located off Saddle Road Hwy. 200, Skyline Trail is accessed between the 43 and 44 mile marker. Turn into the Kilohana Hunters Checking station area. Park here and follow the road most traveled and see map.

Skyline Trail: 10.8 miles one way
Rating: Beginner start, advanced uphill and intermediate downhill
Special: No permits needed
Note: 4WD road
Hazards: Recreational vehicles, high altitude sickness, loose rock and cinder, steep areas and hunters. Harsh weather patterns may set in without warning, including high winds, freezing rain, sleet and snow at the higher elevations.
Amenities: None
History: Old access road primarily used by hunters. During the 1940's, hunting helped to minimize the feral sheep population in this area.
Elevation: 5,500 to 9,900 feet

Skyline Trail is a 4WD road consisting of cinder, dirt, gravel and some rocky sections. The first five miles has a mild grade and is made up of crushed, packed red cinder and gravel, making for excellent mountain biking for riders of all skill levels. Many unmarked smaller roads intersect with Skyline, so use your map and odometer for guidance and stay on the main road.

At 4.2 miles, advanced riders turn right at the Pu'ula'au Ranger Station to access Skyline. Everything beyond the first five miles is for serious uphill "hammer heads" only. At approximately 5.2 miles the road splits. Stay right to challenge the climb to nearly 10,000 feet. Stop along the way to get acclimated and avoid altitude sickness. The ride up is slow going and a grueling cardiovascular experience. Some sections are so steep with

Skyline Trail

Advanced ◆◆◆

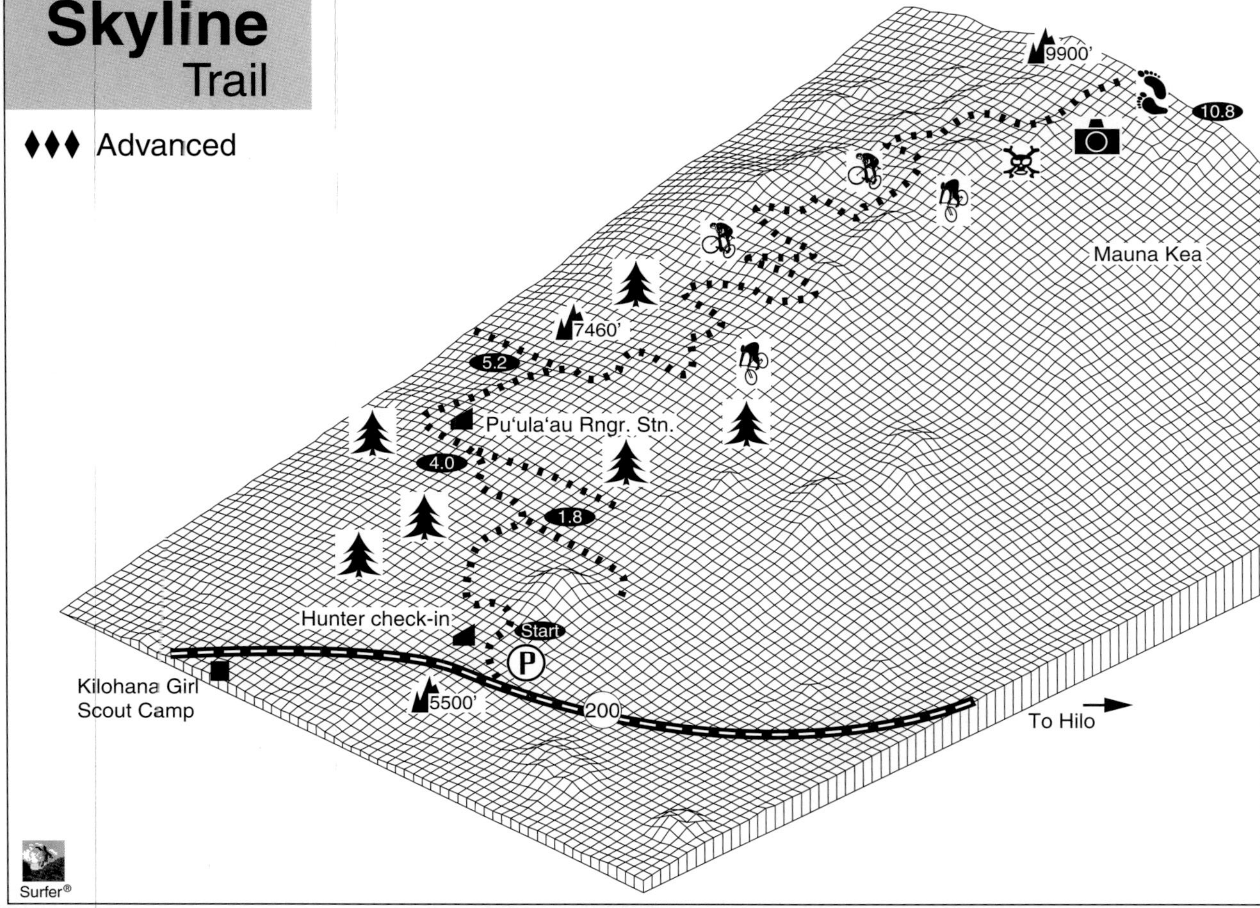

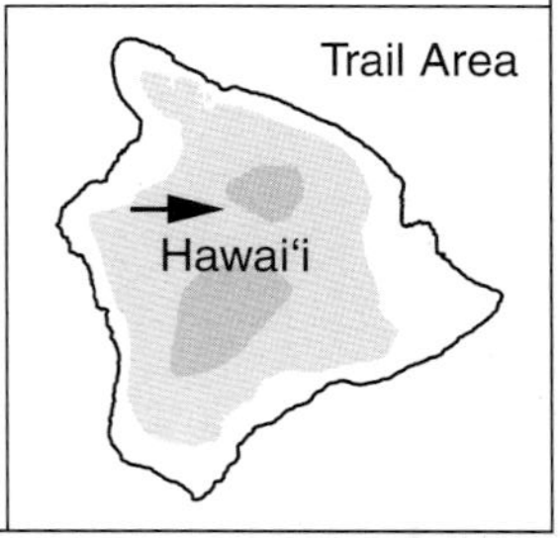

Trail Area

Hawaiʻi

Mauna Kea

To Hilo

10.8

9900'

7460'

5.2

4.0

1.8

Puʻulaʻau Rngr. Stn.

Hunter check-in

Start

P

200'

5500'

Kilohana Girl
Scout Camp

Surfer®

loose top soil that you will have to dismount and walk your bike. Oversized water bars were constructed across the road in an attempt to divert heavy run off during rain storms. These make for exciting launching pads during the downhill. The temperature and weather conditions at this altitude can change dramatically, so be prepared for cold conditions with a chance of high winds, freezing wind, rain sleet and even snow during the winter months.

Before retreating back down, take in the views because you won't have time to look at anything but the road during the downhill. You'll notice only small, high altitude vegetation clinging to life in this cold, volcanic wonderland. The silversword, only found in high elevations of Haleakala, Maui and Mauna Kea are easily spotted with their silvery cactus appearance. Do not disturb them or any of the plants along the road. The black fingers of old lava flows can be seen on neighboring Mauna Loa. Some of the flows were as recent as 1975 and 1984.

For the downhill mountain biker, catching a ride to the top of Skyline in a 4WD will eliminate the harsh 10.8 mile pedal up and provide one of the longest off-road downhills that Hawai'i offers.

Alternate route: Going left at the 5.2 mile mark will also require advanced skills and high endurance. This is an extremely rocky and technical route that encompasses the 7,000 to 9,000 foot level of Mauna Kea's northern slopes ending some 35 miles away at the Ellison Onizuka Astronomy Center off of John A. Burns Highway to the summit. It is a long, difficult ride with loose cinder and rock and many steep climbs, making for extreme mountain biking conditions. This route should only be ridden by advanced riders.

©curt evans 1993

Pine Trees

How to get there: From Kailua-Kona, head north for approximately 7 miles along the Queen Ka'ahumanu Highway 19 towards Keahole Airport. On the makai side of the highway between the 94 and 95 mile markers is the entrance to the Natural Energy Lab. Proceed down approximately one mile to the Wawaloli Beach parking area. The gate is open during the hours posted.

Pine Trees: Approximately 6.4 miles for both trails combined
Rating: Beginner to intermediate
Special: Gates are open between the hours of 6am and 8pm.
Note: Sandy road with exposed lava rock.
Hazards: Vehicles, seasonal high surf and sharp lava rock.
Amenities: Restrooms, showers and pay phone.
History: Old ala kahakai ("trail by the sea"). Ho'ona Historical Preserve along north trail. Contact the Natural Energy Lab (NELHA) at 329-7341 for more information.
Elevation Range: Ocean level

This is a scenic coastal ride that riders of all levels can enjoy. The trail extends south and north along the coast from the parking area.

The north trail is approximately 1.2 miles one way and begins about 50 yards north of the paved parking area. A sign marks the path which is a combination of deep sand and lava terrain.

Trail tip: Speed, momentum and a low tire pressure are recommended for deep sand.

The north trail ends at Ho'ona Historical Preserve. Here are the remains of ancient Hawaiian grave sites, houses and other historical sites, dating from the 1800's.

Enter only as signs permit and lock bikes outside.

Returning south, just past the Wawaloli Beach Park, the trail veers right along the sandy coastal road for approximately 2.0 miles and is better suited for beginners. Here "Pine Trees" is a popular surfing area with the locals. Some swimming spots exist along side this sandy roadway, but use caution during high surf. The road eventually becomes deep sand and is unpassable. Turn around here and enjoy the ride back. Not much shade in this area, so prepare for hot riding conditions.

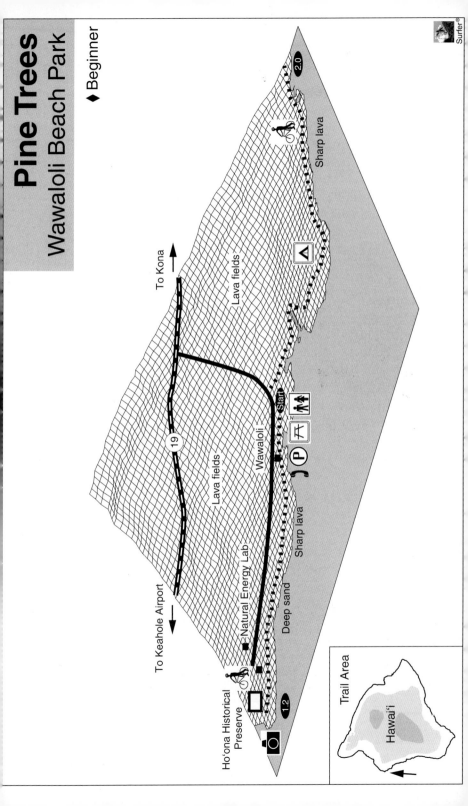

'Ainapo Trail

How to get there: On the southern coast of Hawai'i along Mamalahoa Highway 11, access to 'Ainapo Trail is on the mauka side of the highway between the 40 and 41 mile marker. The brown and yellow Na Ala Hele sign will be at the unlocked gate. Be sure to close all gates after you pass through.

'Ainapo Trail: 8.2 miles one way
Rating: Intermediate to advanced
Special: No permit needed. Close all gates behind you.
Note: 4WD road through pastures of livestock.
Hazards: Cold rain, mud and fog. Hunting where signs are posted. Livestock.
Amenities: Cabin available by permit only. See Appendix.
History: The foot trail from Kapapala is said to be pioneered by ancient Hawaiians who climbed to Mauna Loa's summit to honor the fire goddess Pele.
'Ainapo, lit. "darkened land" because it is often foggy.
Elevation Range: 2,600 to 5,480 feet

This 4WD road starts at approximately 2,600 feet and ascends Mauna Loa through the Kapapala Forest Reserve. The first couple miles of dirt road is mostly rolling pasture lands, becoming steeper and more rugged throughout the climb. No matter how far you actually pedal or walk up, the ride back down is fun and well worth the uphill struggle. Cattle roam free makai of the Kapapala Forest Reserve gate, including bulls, so use caution and don't spook the animals.

Near the three mile mark, on your left is the old abandoned 'Ainapo Ranch House tucked away amongst the tall eucalyptus trees.

Continuing up the arduous hill, you will reach your third

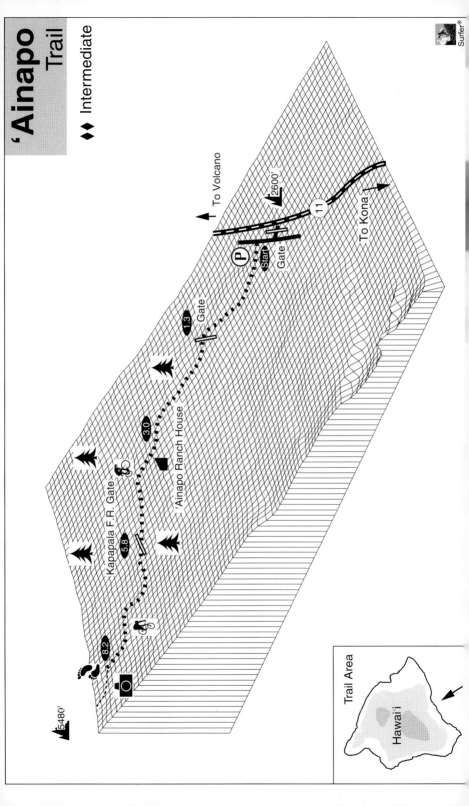

gate which opens into the Kapapala Forest Reserve. Here the road increases in grade and difficulty. On a clear day, you can see Hawai'i Volcanoes National Park some ten miles distance through the clearings. It stands out with its black fingers of barren volcanic wasteland cutting through the dark green forest.

As you proceed, listen to the forest around you. It is alive with the sights and sounds of various native birds, such as the 'elepaio, 'amakihi, 'apapane, and 'i'iwi. These birds can be seen fluttering about among the native 'ohia lehua and koa trees, and a variety of ferns.

This rugged climb ends at 5,480 feet where a historic Hawaiian foot trail begins an ascent to the 13,677 foot summit. No bikes are permitted on the foot trail. Stay on dirt road.

For a cold, yet enjoyable overnight stay, you may lock bikes and hike an additional 2.5 miles to the 7,750 foot elevation to the 'Ainapo trail shelter. This cabin comes with six bunks, mattresses and stools, a table, water (not suitable for drinking without treatment), and a composting toilet. Permits for the cabin must be obtained through the Hawai'i Division of Forestry and Wildlife at 974-4221.

Hawai'i Volcanoes National Park:

On the southeastern slopes of Mauna Loa, the Hawai'i Volcanoes National Park provides riders unlimited excitement and near prehistoric off-road opportunities. Pedal through forests of giant hapu'u tree ferns and ancient 'ohia while passing deep cracks in the earth's crust that billow with steam.

How to get there: Located on the southeastern end of the Big Island, travel south along Mamalahoa Highway 11. Near the 28 mile marker, turn makai into the entrance of Hawai'i Volcanoes National Park. A small fee is required for each car or for each bike if riding in. Annual passes are available by request.

Volcano Trails: Mountain biking within the 230,000 acre Hawai'i Volcanoes National Park is restricted to paved roads and select dirt roads and trails only. Access to mountain bikes is permitted on the following trails.

Due to earthquakes and lava flows, the park terrain is ever changing. Visitors are encouraged to stop at the Kilauea Visitor Center to obtain information on current changes, eruptions and dangers. Contact numbers are located in the Appendix. This is one of the few national parks that allow mountain biking off-road. Ride with respect and tread lightly at all times.

Camping: Camping areas are provided within this national park. Namakani Paio at 4,000 feet provides water, cooking shelter and fireplaces. Kamoamoa, near the ocean, has untreated tap water in the rest room. Campsites are available on a first come basis. Also, inquire with the Volcano House about the rustic cabins available at Namakani Paio. Check with the Kilauea Visitor Center for further information. See Appendix.

Lava facts: Hawai'i's lava is low in silica and gas content, so its high intensity heat creates a less viscous lava, which flows easily and rarely creates explosive releases like that of Mount Saint Helen's in Washington State. Rather, fountains of molten lava with under and above ground lava rivers flow seaward creating paths of fire and destruction. Molten lava reaches extremely hot temperatures up to 2156°F (1180°C). The two common lava types in Hawai'i are the 'a'a and pahoehoe. The 'a'a lava is rough, sharp and bunched up like mountains of broken up rock. The pahoehoe has a smoother, ropy surface and is much easier to walk on once it has cooled. Hiking on new or old lava flows is not recommended, except for areas designated by park officials. Underground lava tubes sometimes have thin ceilings which can collapse, causing sever injury and even death to those walking over them.

All paved roads and highways within the park are open to cars and bicycles unless otherwise noted. Bikes should only be ridden off-road where permitted as indicated below. No single track is allowed within the park, but plenty of excellent double track and dirt roads are available to satisfy the hungry off-road enthusiast.

Caution: Visitors with respiratory problems are advised to use extreme caution near and around the steam and sulphur vents. The "rotten egg" smell is caused by hydrogen sulfide being released through volcanic cracks and fractures in the earth's crust. Always carry your medication in the event of an acute attack of shortness of breath that could occur from sulphuric inhalation in this area. Steam vents release steam with temperatures reaching over 200ºF (93ºC). Visitors are advised to stay on the main trail and behind the safety of the railings near the vents and steep cliffs.

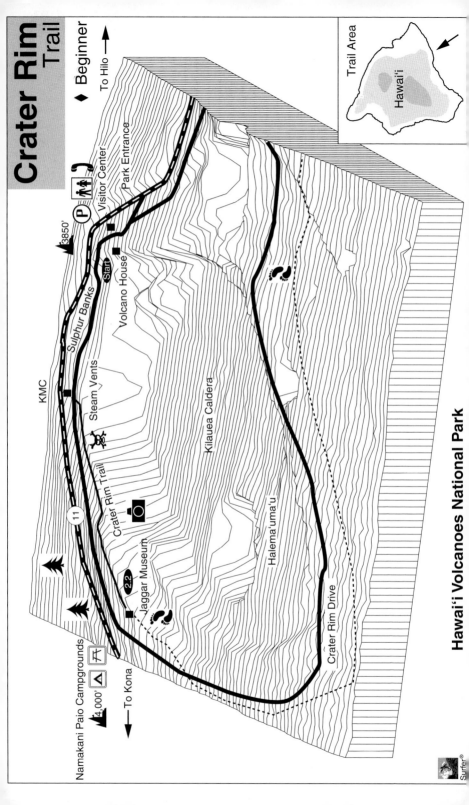

Hawai'i Volcanoes National Park

Crater Rim Trail

How to get there: Park at the Kilauea Visitors Center and ride out of the parking lot to the right along Crater Rim Drive towards the Steam Vents. Follow the narrow paved path on right of road until the Kilauea Military Camp KMC. Cross the street to access the gravel trail. See map.

Crater Rim Trail: Of the 2.2 mile pedal from the Visitors Center to Jaggar Museum, 1.4 miles is a gravel and dirt trail.
Rating: Beginner to advanced
Special: Do not stray off the main trail.
Note: Single track consisting of gravel, cinder and a short paved section.
Hazards: Steep cliffs and loose surface. Steam and sulphur vents. Rapid weather changes. Prepare for cold and wet conditions.
Amenities: None
History: Trail ends at Thomas A. Jaggar Museum and Observatory. Exhibits feature volcanic and seismic information plus, historical and cultural facts of the Hawaiian Islands.
Elevation Range: 3,850 to 3,950 feet

From the Kilauea Visitors Center, turn right onto Crater Rim Drive. Stop to see the colorful mineral deposits from the Sulphur Banks at your first right. Continuing along Crater Rim Drive, don't miss the Steam Vents on your left which pour endless steam clouds into the air.

Crater Rim Trail head starts directly across from KMC and veers right following the southwestern edge of Kilauea Caldera. Stay right at the fork and follow the trail along the western edge of the Kilauea Caldera. This gravel and cinder path continues west along the scenic 'Uwekahuna Bluff which harbors steep cliffs some 400 feet above the caldera floor. Eerie views of the steaming caldera and Halema'uma'u Crater in the distance provide a constant reminder of the awesome power of mother nature. The spectacular sites and historical aspects of this area are what make this ride so unique. Kilauea Caldera is 2.5 miles long and 2 miles wide and was formed by series of collapses over hundreds of years. It was twice as deep as it is today in the late 1700's and early 1800's. The trail ends at the Jaggar Museum which offers educational facts about the volcano, including the geology, history and culture of the Hawaiian Islands.

Escape Road

How to get there: You may start from the Thurston Lava Tube which is approximately one mile from the Visitor Center on Crater Rim Drive. From Thurston Lava Tube, follow the paved path up to the right and proceed through the small gate to access Escape Road.

From outside the park, access is from the makai side of Highway 11, directly across from Old Volcano Road. Pass the gated entrance and follow the trail .25 mile to reach Escape Road. Turn left and follow the cinder road .75 mile to Thurston Lava Tube. Proceed beyond the informational signs and continue on Escape Road through another gated entrance.

Escape Road: 4 miles one way from Thurston Lava Tube.
Rating: Beginner to advanced
Special: No permit needed.
Note: 4WD road
Hazards: Bumpy and sharp cinder road. Possible vehicular traffic. Rapid weather changes. Prepare for cold and wet conditions.
Amenities: None
History: Built in 1885 as Keauhou Road, it was used to shuttle park visitors and supplies via horse and carriage to the boat landing at Keauhou. In 1963, Hawai'i Volcanoes National Park restored it as an Escape Road. Crosses a portion of a 1973 lava flow near Pauahi Crater.
Elevation Range: 3,835 to 3,150 feet

Escape Road is a mountain bikers dream and another great testing ground for your full suspension bike. It is a grated cinder road that is completely surrounded by giant hapu'u tree ferns, 'ohia and a variety of fern undergrowth.

If you begin this ride from Thurston Lava Tube, enter the paved entrance and proceed left to find a short .75 mile cinder road through lush Hawaiian rainforest. Escape Road will intersect Crater Rim Drive near the park entrance. Double back to the lava tube to begin the downhill.

While at Thurston Lava Tube, don't miss an unforgettable walking tour that descends a native rainforest of giant hapu'u tree ferns to

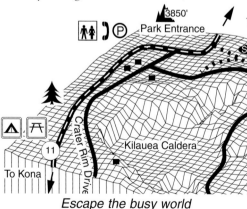

Escape the busy world and experience Escape Road.

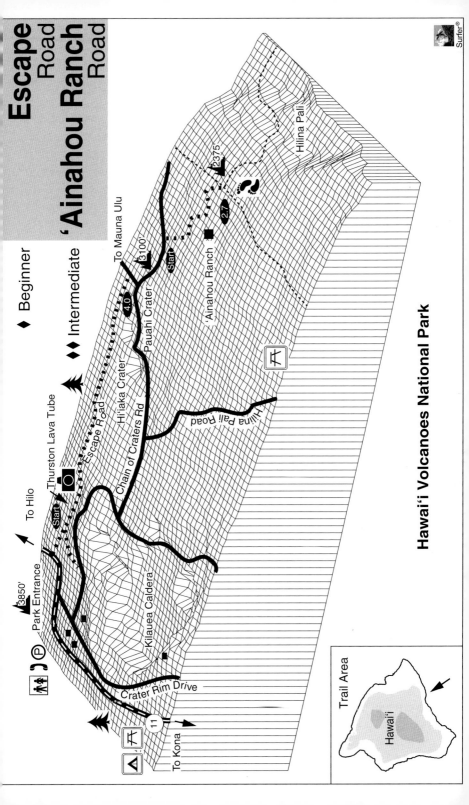

Escape Road
'Ainahou Ranch Road

◆ Beginner

◆◆ Intermediate

Hawai'i Volcanoes National Park

Trail Area

Hawai'i

Surfer®

the entrance of a 450 foot lava tube that is near 20 feet in height in some spots. As you walk along this paved route, you will be awestruck of the reality that this lava cylinder was once flowing with a stream of molten 2,000 degree lava. Bring a lock for your bike.

For the maximum tropical downhill thrill, go right at the paved entrance to the lava tube. You will have to pass a gate to continue. Be sure to close all gates behind you. Follow the cinder road down for 4 miles through lush native Hawaiian rainforest. At approximately 3.3 miles, the forest canopy opens up to a lava flow from 1973. After passing through this lava flow, Escape Road ends near Mauna Ulu. Go left along the paved road just .5 mile to see Mauna Ulu, a 350 foot high volcanic shield. Mauna Ulu means "growing mountain". Mauna Ulu was active from 1969 - 1974 and had grown two-thirds its present size in just one year.

From here, you can ride back up the Escape Road or Crater Rim Drive. Or, continue your adventure to 'Ainahou Ranch Road, if time and energy permits. See map. Have fun on the ride back up!

'Ainahou Ranch Road

How to get there: Heading down the Chain of Craters Road, turn right between the 4 and 5 mile markers. The trail begins just beyond the gated entry to 'Ainahou Ranch Road. See map.

'Ainahou Ranch Road: 5.4 miles round trip
Rating: Intermediate to advanced
Special: No permit needed
Note: 4WD road.
Hazards: Lava rocks and uneven terrain. Possible vehicular traffic. Dramatic weather changes can occur. Prepare for cold rain, wind and fog.
Amenities: None
History: Access road to the 'Ainahou Ranch home built during the late 1930's by Herbert Shipman. *'Ainahou,* lit. "new land".
Elevation Range: 3,100 - 2,375 feet

Proceed around the gated entrance and continue along the dirt and gravel road. This is an old access road to the 'Ainahou Ranch. As you proceed, you will encounter forks in the road at approximately 1.0 mile and 1.6 miles. Stay left at the intersections and follow the road most traveled.

At approximately 2.7 miles, 'Ainahou Ranch Road ends at the intersection of Keauhou Trail, Chain of Craters and Halape Trail. Bicycles are prohibited beyond this point due to the endangered nene geese. Riders must turn around and proceed back up 'Ainahou Ranch Road to your starting position.

Bike Tours - Big Island

The Big Island of Hawai'i has bicycle tours that will take you to from mauka to makai. With so many miles to cover, you can choose from mild country roads to a kamikaze downhill from the highest peak in the state.

The following lists some of the companies providing organized tours.

Bike Hawaii - Summit to the Sea

Bike Hawaii takes you on a guided multi-day mountain bike adventure from the cool slopes of Mauna Kea to the warm sandy beaches that embrace the Pacific Ocean. Rustic cabin accommodations and tent camping make for an island experience you'll never forget. These multi-day adventures are tailored to meet the interests of each group.

Trips include ground transportation, all meals and accommodations. Explore Hawai'i with Bike Hawaii. Trips are customized and offered with strict minimums by request only. See Appendix for contact information.

Mauna Kea Mountain Bikes

Mauna Kea Mountain Bikes is one of the island's best bicycle tour operations with genuine aloha. Mauna Kea Mountain Bikes will pick you up at your hotel and provide all the necessary safety equipment and bikes.

Since 1993, owner Grant Mitchell has lead bike tours through the scenic and unspoiled beauty of Hawai'i. Tours are tailored to accommodate all skill levels. Skilled riders may choose the screamin' kamikaze downhill from the 13,796 foot summit of Mauna Kea to the 6,400 foot base. Only 4 miles of crushed cinder off-roading and the rest is paved and fast.

For a more relaxed biking adventure, knowledgeable tour guides will lead you down the upper highway of the North Kohala mountains to Hawi with beautiful panoramic views of ranch lands and the island of Maui across the 'Alenuihaha Channel. Mauna Kea Mountain Bikes is the right connection for mauna biking! See the Appendix for contact numbers.

Club Rides

The Big Island Mountain Bike Association (BIMBA) is a nonprofit organization.. BIMBA's goal is to promote the sport of mountain biking as well as other trail activity programs which include the development of training and safety programs: coordinating agreements and permits to establish suitable riding trails; and the development and distribution of important information on the use of state and/or private trails. BIMBA strongly supports the growth of mountain biking in a responsible manner and is committed to reducing potential user conflicts. BIMBA also offers ongoing activities such as fun rides, races and trail maintenance.

If you would like to get involved with any of BIMBA's mountain bike rides or other activities, call them and inquire about upcoming events. A contact number is in the Appendix.

Maui - The Valley Isle

Maui is the second largest of the Hawaiian Islands and is 48 miles long and 26 miles wide. Maui is made up of two mountains, the West Maui Mountains and Haleakala. Haleakala ("house of the sun") is a massive volcano which stands at 10,023 feet. It is the third highest mountain peak in the state, and its crater is approximately 2,500 feet deep and 7.5 miles wide. Haleakala is considered to be a dormant volcano, having last erupted in 1790, when the lava flow created La Perouse Bay on Maui's southwest shoreline.

Haleakala National Park, located on the summit, is often snow covered during winter storms and is known for its magnificent sunrises, nene geese and rare silversword plants. Haleakala is also very

popular for its downhill bicycle tours which are restricted to the 28 mile paved highway leading to the summit. Mountain biking is not allowed within the crater, however, plenty of hiking and backpacking opportunities are available. During storms, call the summit report at 572-7749 before attempting the rigorous climb.

After you've seen the beaches, survived the long, winding road to Hana and spent your paycheck in the old whaling town of Lahaina, it's time to head for the hills. When you hunger for pristine single track, look no further. Gear up and head straight for Polipoli in the 4,965 acre Kula Forest Reserve on the slopes of Haleakala. At 6,000 feet, riders enjoy cool, alpine style riding conditions on miles of legal single track and 4WD roads. Camping is available at Polipoli State Park for those overnighter trips, when one day of riding just isn't enough.

The tropical coastlines and deep valleys where waterfalls are plentiful are what makes Maui unforgettable. There is a saying in Hawai'i, "Maui, no ka oi", "Maui is the best". One trip to Maui and you'll be saying it, too!

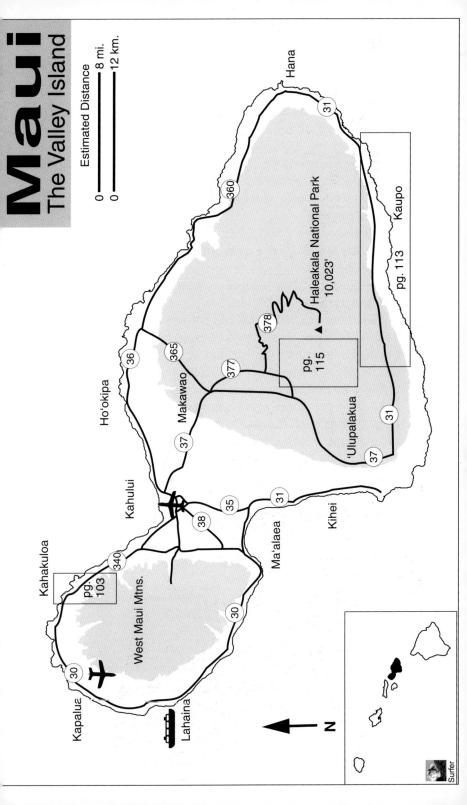

Kahakuloa

How to get there: Take Kahekili Highway 340 from either direction around the West Maui mountains. Between the 40 and 41 mile marker, turn up at the Kahakuloa Game Management Area (GMA) Access sign.

Kahakuloa: Approximately 5 miles one way
Rating: Intermediate to advanced
Special: GMA. Stay on main road and do not stray onto hunting trails. Wear bright colored clothing.
Note: 4WD road.
Hazards: Vehicular traffic, loose roots and rocks. Hunting.
Amenities: None
History: Old access road for hunting. *Kahakuloa,* lit. "the tall lord"
Elevation Range: 370 to 2,000+ feet

Kahakuloa is an excellent uphill and downhill training ground for experienced riders. This area is used by hunters, so riders should exercise caution by riding on the main road only and wearing bright colored clothing.

From the entrance gate near the Poʻelua hunters check-in station, it is a steady hill climb to the second gate, approximately 1.75 miles away. The vistas from the upper ridgeline are unbeatable. Eastern Molokaʻi is easily seen across the Pailololo Channel. On the right side below the ridge trail is Honokahau Stream. It stretches for miles up towards Puʻu Kukui, the highest point of the West Maui Mountains at 5,788 feet. Often times this gulch is hiding in the mist from the rainy summits above.

From the second gate, you may proceed beyond the pine forest to the border of the Natural Area Reserve (NAR). Beautiful green grassy pastures cover the upper ridgeline near the 2,000 foot mark. No bicycles are permitted into the NAR area. From here, riders may turn around and double back down the same path you came up. Certain sections may seem steeper going down than they did coming up. Proceed slowly and use caution in the corners. Have fun!

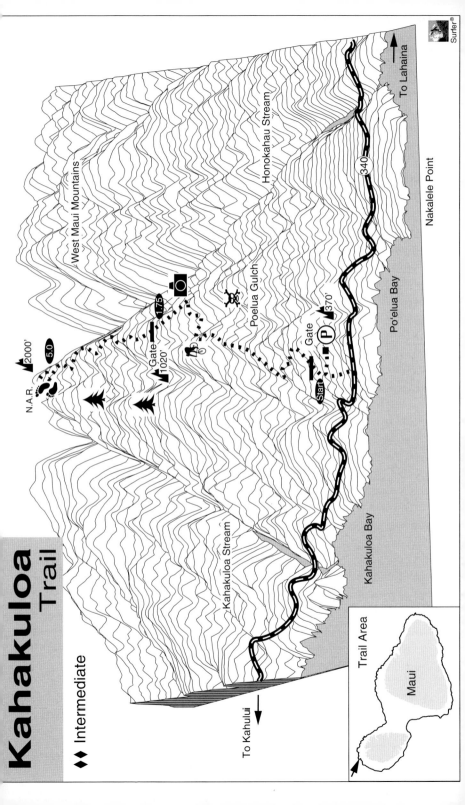

Kaupo Road

How to get there: Kaupo Road is accessed from either Hana or 'Ulupalakua. From 'Ulupalakua, pass the 20 acre Tedeschi Vineyards along Pi'ilani Highway 31 and proceed approximately 19 miles east until the paved highway ends. The dirt road marks the beginning of Kaupo Road.

Kaupo Road: 4.5 miles one way
Rating: Beginner to advanced
Special: Public access road. No permit needed.
Note: Unkept coastal dirt road.
Hazards: Vehicular traffic, stream crossing and steep cliffs.
Amenities: None
History: Sites include St. Joseph Church (1862) and Hui Aloha Church (1859). *Kaupo*, lit. "landing [of canoes] at night"
Elevation Range: Sea level to 100 feet

Along the scenic highway which covers the southeastern coastal point of Maui, there is a 4.5 mile section of road that is unpaved and fun for mountain biking. This serpentine road is at the base of the Kaupo Gap which extends up to Haleakala Crater. Kaupo Road is perhaps one of the most scenic rides on the island, with ocean views and mauka vistas that will take your breath away. Pass historic Kaupo and visit some of Maui's oldest churches, the St. Joseph Church (since 1862) and the Hui Aloha Church (since 1859). Stop at the historic Kaupo Store and see what country living is all about. Just two miles ahead, you will need to cross a flowing stream, but use caution during strong flows or when it's raining.

Beginning this ride from 'Ulupalakua, riders experience panoramic views of the forbidden island of Kaho'olawe and diving favorite, Molokini Island. As you descend, the landscape goes through dramatic changes from lava fields and a barren coastline to the lush tropical forests with virtually every shade of green and refreshing Hawaiian waterfalls. Starting elevation is approximately 3,000 feet and descends to sea level. For a more relaxed adventure, rent a vehicle and have someone follow you around to the other side and pick you up when you're pau.

On both sides of Pi'ilani Highway, you will encounter thousands of acres of private land belonging to Department of Hawaiian Home Lands (DHHL) and Kaupo Ranch. Stay on the main road and watch for the occasional car you will encounter. Sometimes you may run across stray cattle, so be prepared to stop or pass the animals slowly.

Some experienced riders choose to pedal the entire length from Tedeschi Vineyards in 'Ulupalakua to Hana and back. Others, will complete the ride around the entire base of Haleakala and back to their original starting position. This ride is long and taxing and requires a rider with the stamina and endurance to complete the round trip.

Iron Fist, Moloka'i Ranch

Keoki Trail, Moloka'i Ranch.

Moloka'i Forest Reserve.

The view of Kalaupapa from Na'iwa, Moloka'i Ranch.

Descending Haleakala via Skyline, Maui.

View toward Moʻomomi from Naʻiwa, Molokaʻi Ranch.

Polipoli State Park, Maui.

Mamane Trail, Maui.

Another day in paradise, Lanaʻi

Polipoli Access Road, Maui.

Munro Trail, Lanaʻi.

Historical Kaunolu, Lanaʻi.

Descending Makakupaʻia, Molokaʻi.

Waikolu Valley Overlook, Molokaʻi.

Puu o Hoku Ranch, Moloka'i

Ho'okipa, Maui.

Traveling twice the speed of sound, it's easy to get burned.

Polihua Road to Lana'i City.

Going crazy in the garden, Lana'i.

Shadow riders of Moloka'i.

Kaupo
Road

◆ Beginner

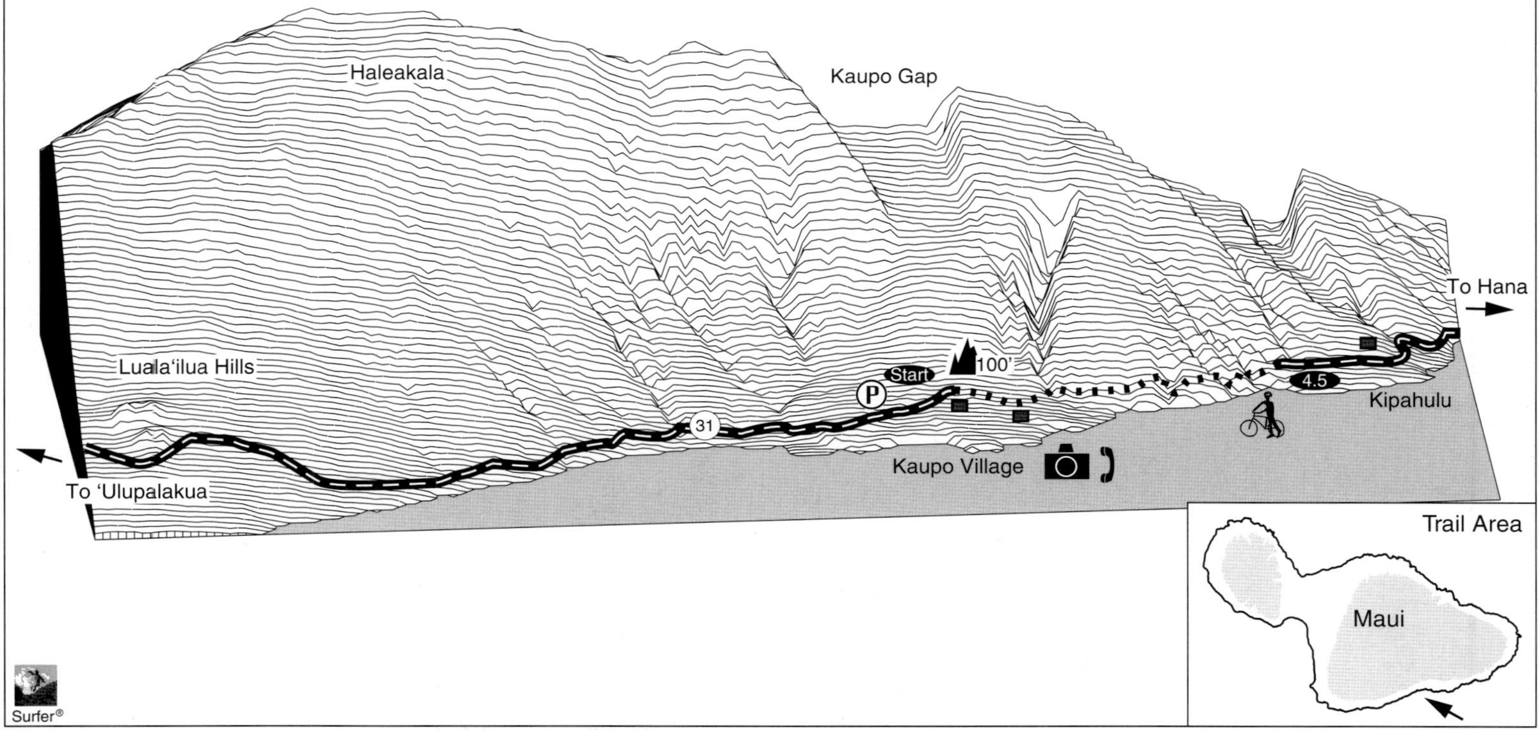

Trail Area

Maui

To Hana

Kipahulu

4.5

Kaupo Gap

100'

Start

P

Kaupo Village

31

Haleakala

Luala'ilua Hills

To 'Ulupalakua

Surfer®

Kula Forest Reserve: Polipoli Access Road

How to get there: From Kahului, take Highway 37 south up country towards Kula. Between the 13 and 14 mile marker, turn left onto Highway 377 east and make your first right onto Waipoli Road. You will pass through private ranch land and over a series of cattle guards to get to the forest reserve. You will pass the hunters check-in station at the entrance to Waiakoa Loop Trail just 5 miles up. See map.

Proceed up Waipoli Road another mile to where it becomes a dirt road known as Polipoli Access Road. You may park here to begin your ride, or drive in another 3.5 miles to Polipoli State Park.

Polipoli Access Road: 5.4 miles one way
Rating: Beginner to advanced
Special: All trails downslope of the dirt road are off-limits to mountain bikes and are for hiking only. See map.
Note: 4WD road when wet.
Hazards: Prepare for cold and wet conditions. Dress warmly. Steep acclivity with cliff areas after first 5 miles.
Amenities: Polipoli State Park offers one cabin and campgrounds by permit only. Parking, shelter, potable water and flushing toilet also available.
History: 1950's access road to the Haleakala summit observatories, referred to then as "Science City".
Elevation Range: 6,100 to 6,800 feet

This semi-level dirt road is a perfect training ground for beginners for the first 4.2 miles in. Once you have passed Polipoli State Park, it is less than one mile to where the road makes a sharp u-turn and increases in grade and difficulty. Beginners are advised to turn around here, or proceed to test your endurance level.

Polipoli Access Road winds through a variety of introduced trees including, redwood, cedar and pine, creating an environment similar to that of Northern California. The cool temperature and smell of fresh pine creates an illusion that you are far from the tropical hills of Hawai'i.

Camping at Polipoli State Park is a great way to enjoy multiple days of mountain biking on the slopes of the dormant Haleakala volcano. From the campgrounds, intermediate and advanced riders

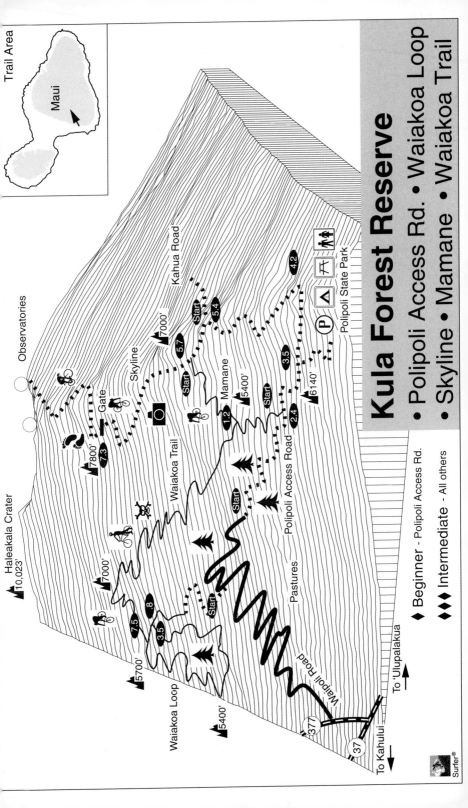

Kula Forest Reserve

- Polipoli Access Rd. • Waiakoa Loop
- Skyline • Mamane • Waiakoa Trail

Trail Area

Maui

Observatories

Haleakala Crater
10,023'

Kahua Road

Skyline

Gate

7800'

7.3

7000'

Waiakoa Trail

Mamane

Start 5.7

Start 5.4

Start 4.2

7000'

5400'

Start 1.2

Start 2.4

Start 3.5

6140'

Polipoli Access Road

Polipoli State Park

Start

Pastures

Start

Waiakoa Loop

7.5

3.5

.8

5700'

5400'

Start

Waipoli Road

377

37

To Kahului

To 'Ulupalakua

◆ Beginner - Polipoli Access Rd.

◆◆ Intermediate - All others

Surfer®

can access the single track of Mamane Trail and Waiakoa Trail, or climb the arduous road to Skyline. See map.

While at the park, don't miss hiking the beautiful trails. Brilliant green ferns blanket the ground at the base of towering pine forests. Often times, misty clouds will hover along the trail while beams of sunlight penetrate the forest canopy and provide dramatic lighting effects.

Waiakoa Loop Trail

How to get there: The Waiakoa Loop Trail is located just 5 miles up Waipoli Road from Highway 377. Park at the hunter check-in station. Proceed to the end of the .8 mile 4WD access road to begin the Waiakoa Loop Trail. Stay on the main road and do not stray onto private land and hunting trails. You will need to pass through a gate to enter the forest reserve. Be sure to close the gate behind you. Waiakoa Loop can also be accessed via the Waiakoa Trail. See map.

Waiakoa Loop Trail: 4.3 miles round trip from hunter station
Rating: Intermediate to advanced
Special: Crosses section of private land. Stay on main road.
Note: Single track and 4WD road.
Hazards: Steep and slippery in some sections. Rocks, roots, washouts and cliffs are prevalent. Prepare for cold and wet conditions. Warm clothes are recommended.
Amenities: None
History: Old hunting trail, rebuilt as public hiking/biking trail. *Waiakoa,* lit. "water [used] by warrior"
Elevation Range: 5,700 to 5,400 feet

Waiakoa Loop Trail is a beautiful mountain biking adventure through pristine Kula Forest. A short .8 mile road through private ranch land will lead you to the forest reserve gate. Once you have entered the gate, the trail starts off with a mild climb leading to a fork in the trail. This is the beginning of the 3 mile loop. Going straight is recommended for a fun and challenging serpentine downhill through pine and a variety of timberland trees. Just ahead approximately .5 mile, you will note the intersection of the Waiakoa Trail on your right which leads to Polipoli Access Road some 7.5 miles away. Read the Waiakoa Trail text for more information.

The trail is narrow in some sections and has occasional rocky riverbed crossings. Use caution near the cliffs that exist and don't cross streambeds if the water level is high. Trail markers indicate mileage from the start of the loop.

The single track leads you to a hidden world of mountain biking opportunity. After reaching the bottom, a steep uphill grade will test your strength and endurance. You may have to dismount and walk your bike in the steep technical sections. Complete the loop again for double the fun. Enjoy!

Waiakoa Trail

How to get there: Access is from Polipoli Access Road just 1.1 miles from the entrance to Polipoli State Park. Access is also from the Waiakoa Loop Trail. See map.

Waiakoa Trail: Approximately 7.5 miles one way
Rating: Intermediate to advanced
Special: Unfinished trail. Crosses section of private land. Check with Na Ala Hele. See Appendix for contact number.
Note: Single track. Trail head marker on Polipoli Access Road might indicate it as Upper Waiohuli Trail. This is the correct entrance to Waiakoa Trail.
Hazards: Steep, rocky and narrow trail with some cliff areas. Prepare for cold and wet conditions.
Amenities: None
History: Old hunting trail, rebuilt as public hiking, biking and horse trail.

Waiakoa, lit. "water [used] by warrior".

Elevation Range: 6,190 to 7,000 feet

Waiakoa Trail intersects with the Waiakoa Loop Trail, Mamane Trail and Polipoli Access Road. See map.

Starting this trail form Polipoli Access Road, Waiakoa begins as a steady uphill climb over a pine forest trail covered with a blanket of pine needles. You might encounter other mountain bikers coming down from the Mamane Trail which begins from Skyline. At the the junction of Mamane Trail, you will notice an old volcanic pu'u (hill) on your right that offers some interesting photo opportunities. Stay left at this junction and continue up the Waiakoa Trail.

On clear days, you can see for miles. Looking back, you can see from Kihei to Ma'alaea on the southwestern shore, and from Kahului to Wailuku on the northeastern edge of the island.

Proceed up across numerous dry lava riverbeds. You may need to walk your bike in certain areas that are unridable. A foot path with mileage markers will eventually connect you to the Waiakoa Loop Trail. Go left to return to Waipoli Road or double back to your starting position. See map.

Mamane Trail

How to get there: Mamane Trail is accessed as a downhill from Skyline. See map.

Mamane Trail: 1.2 miles one way

Rating: Intermediate to advanced

Special: Best accessed as a downhill from Skyline. See map.

Note: Single track.

Hazards: Rocks and off-camber sections. Prepare for wet and cold conditions.

Amenities: None

History: Trail was cleared in cooperation with the Maui Mountain Bike Club and Na Ala Hele in 1995. Mamane is named after the native tree which thrives in this area.

Elevation Range: 7,000 to 6,500 feet

The Mamane Trail is an alluring single track through the cool Kula Forest Reserve. Often foggy and misty, Mamane Trail is a pristine taste of alpine style single track. Descending from Skyline just above the tree line, this downhill roller coaster has excellent turns and unforgettable views. Obviously designed with the mountain biker in mind, Mamane Trail is guaranteed to please even the most skilled veteran riders. Trail markers were installed during 1996 to help riders with distance calculations. The thrill of this trail will bring you back time and time again.

The trail ends in a lush pine forest adjacent to an old lava pu'u. Here, the trail intersects with the Waiakoa Trail. Going straight will take you .6 mile down to Polipoli Access Road. Going right onto Waiakoa Trail will eventually lead you to the Waiakoa Loop Trail, nearly 7 miles away. See map.

Skyline

How to get there: Proceed up past Polipoli State Park for approximately 2 miles to Ballpark Junction. Stay left to access Skyline. From Ballpark Junction, Kahua Road continues right for approximately 3.5 miles, but becomes private property of DHHL where entry is strictly prohibited.

Skyline: 2.0 miles one way from Ballpark Junction
Rating: Intermediate to advanced
Special: Restricted use beyond the gated entry to the summit.
Note: 4WD road.
Hazards: Steep, rocky, loose and uneven terrain with soft shoulders and cliff areas. Possible vehicular traffic. Prepare for unpredictable winds with wet and cold weather conditions.
Amenities: None
History: 1950's access road to the Haleakala summit observatories, referred to then as "Science City".
Elevation Range: 6,800 to 7,800 feet

"Fire it Up" with this uphill, as Skyline will truly put the heat on your legs. But, at this elevation, it's cool year round. The weather conditions up here can change rapidly and blow excessively strong winds and freezing rain, so dress appropriately. Skyline is above the tree line, offering spectacular views from Kihei to Kahului on the central plain of Maui. Across the 'Alalakeiki Channel are postcard views of Molokini and Kaho'olawe from this elevation, providing picture perfect back drops from anywhere.

At 7,800 feet, an access gate is locked across the road. From this point, it is approximately 5 miles to the 10,023 foot Haleakala summit. Access is restricted because of the nesting grounds for the native nene and petrel, along with the protected silversword which live nowhere else in the world except Hawai'i.

There is an eerie silence at this altitude. Nothing to hear but the beating of your heart and the sound of your tires rolling on the crushed cinder road. Temperatures drop significantly, especially with wet and windy conditions, so prepare yourself ahead of time.

Hold on tight during your descent, for the ride will be fast going and will require your undivided attention to the road. Enjoy!

Bike Tours - Maui

The island of Maui has a variety of bicycle tour operations. The most popular of any tour is the 38 mile downhill from the 10,023 foot elevation of Haleakala. Technically, it is not mountain biking, since the group is restricted to a paved highway. However, many customers find the experience thrilling and fulfilling.

Maui Mountain Cruisers caters to cycling enthusiasts of all ages and riding skills. Their tour comes complete with a continental breakfast, lunch, van transportation to to the top of Haleakala and return from Pa'ia, the downhill bike, helmet and other related equipment. Visitors to Haleakala be advised that temperatures on the summit can be as low as 30 degrees during the summer, so dress in layered clothes that can be stripped down as you descend to a warmer sea level near 85 degrees.

Once the freezing sunrise has been photographed by global visitors, the group gears up and heads out for a 38 mile summit to the sea experience. Maui Mountain Cruisers tour leaders adhere to strict safety rules and descend the mountain at a relatively safe speed for all to enjoy.

The 5 hour ride includes a sit down meal in Kula. The pack then heads out for their final descent to Pa'ia town where the chaser van will pick you and your bike up and return you to Kahului. An enjoyable adventure for the whole family. Don't forget your camera. This ride will take you through a variety of landscapes and green pastures with exceptional views of upcountry Maui. See Appendix for contact numbers.

Club Rides

With the vast amount of land on the island of Maui, it has the potential to be a mountain biking mecca. However, as you will see, trails open to mountain bikes are somewhat limited.

Maui Mountain Bike Club can offer fun rides and races that are sure to please riders of all skill levels. This group of knowledgeable island riders have a lot of aloha and are a pleasure to ride with.

Aside from the many fun rides and off-road events, you can often times find this group of trail lovers out of their saddles maintaining the various mountain biking trails in the Kula area. Club member, Tom Armstrong and his mighty trail crew work closely with Na Ala Hele and have a comradery that is second to none.

To find out about upcoming events , trail maintenance and fun rides, contact the Maui Mountain Bike Club. Their address is in the Appendix.

Moloka'i - The Friendly Island

Home to just over 6,700 residents, Moloka'i, is truly the most Hawaiian island. It has been nicknamed "The Friendly Island" because of the genuine warmth and aloha of the native Hawaiian people. With no traffic lights or parking meters, this 260 sq. mile island is fifth largest, 38 miles long and 10 miles wide. The rugged windward coastline is home to the world's highest sea cliffs which endlessly pour waterfalls from their cloudy summits.

Moloka'i is small enough so that you can easily ride from one end to the other if you are in moderate shape. The highest mountain peak is Kamakou at 4,961 feet, but is only accessed by mountain bike to approximately the 3,700 foot level within the Kamakou Preserve.

Moloka'i has minimal state trails open to mountain bikes, so camping should be considered in the misty forest at Waikolu Campground. Here, riders can enjoy the perfect overnight anticipation of multiple days of mountain biking action within this lush tropical forest reserve.

Moloka'i is an island to remember. While you are there, visit the rest of the island and take in some of the historical sites. Be sure to stop in and say "aloha" to the gang at Moloka'i Bicycle. Owner and life long resident, Phillip Kikukawa is Moloka'i's bicycle specialist and is a wealth of information. While in Kaunakakai, try the famous sweet bread and french bread baked fresh daily at Kanemitsu's Bakery. Stop by Coffees of Hawai'i in Kualapu'u for a fresh cup of their Muleskinner or Maunalani Estate java which is grown fresh in the surrounding hills. Take a mule ride to the remote peninsula of Kalaupapa, the former home of Father Damien who devoted his life to this tiny colony of native Hawaiians with Hansen's Disease (leprosy) during the late 19th century. This isolated village is located at the base of a 1,600 foot rugged northern seacliff.

Moloka'i is unique and is a must for riders who wish to taste a bit of old Hawai'i. You won't find bright city lights or late night dance clubs, just a Hawaiian lifestyle with genuine aloha from its people.

Historic Halawa Valley, Moloka'i

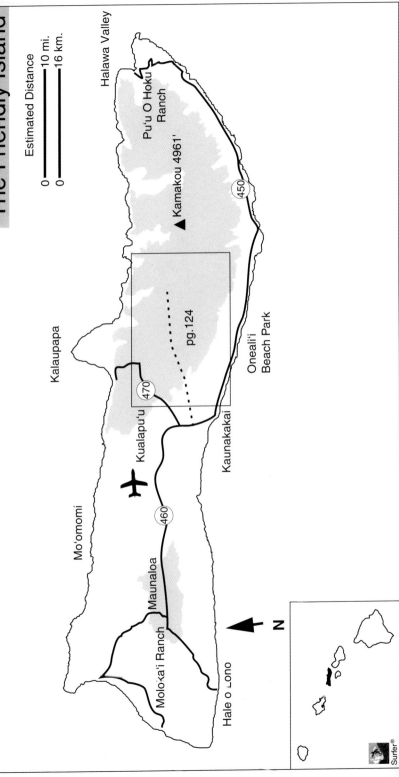

Moloka'i
The Friendly Island

Estimated Distance

0 ———— 10 mi.
0 ———— 16 km.

Halawa Valley

Pu'u O Hoku Ranch

▲ Kamakou 4961'

450

Kalaupapa

pg. 124

Kualapu'u

470

Oneali'i
Beach Park

Kaunakakai

Mo'omomi

460

Maunaloa

Moloka'i Ranch

Hale o Lono

N

Surfer®

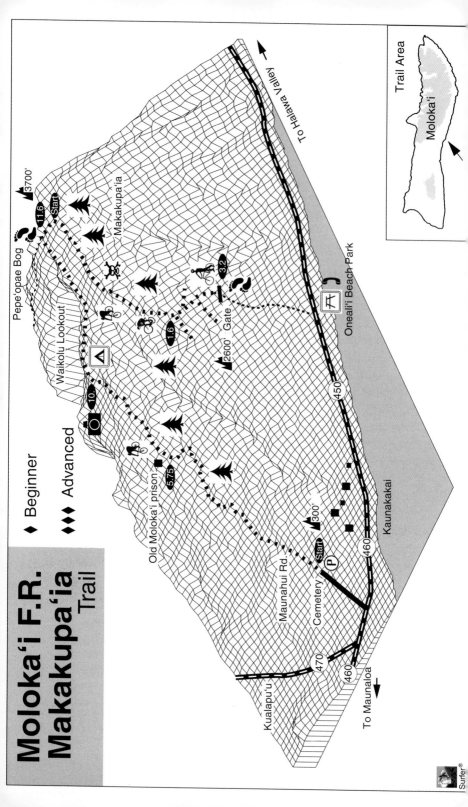

Moloka'i Forest Reserve:

How to get there: From Kaunakakai, go west on Maunaloa Highway 460. Between the 3 and 4 mile markers, turn right just south of the bridge at the Homelani Cemetery sign. This is Maunahui Road, but the street sign may not be present. Approximately .25 mile up this paved road, the cemetery will be on your left. Go straight to begin the 10 mile dirt road that leads to Moloka'i Forest Reserve and Kamakou Preserve.

Moloka'i Forest Reserve: 10 miles one way to Waikolu Lookout
Rating: Beginner to advanced
Special: No permit needed, unless camping overnight.
Note: 4WD dirt road. Wet ride okay.
Hazards:4WD and all terrain vehicles. Slippery when wet. Hunting area.
Amenities: Camping and restrooms at Waikolu Campground by permit only. Water at the old prison grounds.
History: Sandalwood measuring pit and remnants of the Moloka'i's prison in the 1920's.
Elevation Range: 300 to 3,700 feet

This is Moloka'i's best public mountain bike ride and rates high among the list of Hawai'i's best. You will begin this long and grueling ride from approximately 300 feet and slowly pedal up Maunahui Road. This dirt road consists of mud or hard pack. You will pedal to approximately 3,700 feet in just eleven miles. An intermediate rider in decent shape should take approximately two hours to complete the climb. Beginners may opt to stay in the lower foothills which has a milder grade, or challenge the entire climb to W a i k o l u Lookout.

The Moloka'i Forest Reserve has some wild

game animals, including pig, axis deer, and fowl. You are most likely to see the axis deer along your journey. Shade is minimal during the first five miles of your ride, so bring plenty of water and start early to avoid the mid-day sun and heat.

Your ascent will take you up through various levels of mountain vegetation, beginning with dry kiawe forest at the lower elevations, turning to tall eucalyptus and Cook Pines surrounded by 'uluhe fern and 'ohia lehua in the higher elevations of this lush forest reserve.

At approximately 5.75 miles on your left is the former Moloka'i Prison used in the 1920's, but known now as a forestry camp. Here, drinking water can be obtained from an outdoor faucet before continuing further.

At approximately 10 miles, you will reach the Waikolu Valley Lookout on your left. Breathtaking waterfalls are visible in the back of the valley along with spectacular views of the blue ocean and the tiny island of 'Okala, which rises out of the sea at the mouth of the valley. The deep blue of the vast Pacific Ocean provides a dramatic contrast against the dark green of the valley. Stop and listen to the sounds of ancient Hawai'i, as native birds flutter from tree to tree.

Proceeding another 1.6 miles further into the Kamakou Preserve, the road has short and fast downhills with slow going uphills through lush tropical rainforest. At 11.6 miles, the road splits. Bicycles are strictly prohibited beyond this point, and may be locked at your own risk. A road to the right leads down Makakupa'ia Trail to the forest reserve boundary. Riders must turn around here or proceed down Makakupa'ia Trail. See map.

Walk up another mile to the end of the road where a hiking trail leads into the misty Pepe'opae Bog. This area is fenced in to protect its rare eco-system. Here, 250 rare plants live in a delicate rainforest, and 219 are found nowhere else on earth. The Kamakou Preserve is also home to several endangered Hawaiian birds, including the oloma'o and the kakawaihie. A thirty minute walk over the wooden boardwalk will provide astonishing vistas of the rugged north Moloka'i coastline.

Beginner riders should return on the same path that they rode up. Intermediate and advanced riders may proceed down the Makakupa'ia Trail. See text.

Makakupa'ia Trail

How to get there: Pedal up via Maunahui Road through the Moloka'i Forest Reserve and into the Kamakou Preserve. Access to the Makakupa'ia Trail is on the right near the 11.6 mile mark.

Makakupa'ia Trail: 6.4 miles out and back
Rating: Advanced
Special: Cuts through private lands. Stay on main road.
Notes: Rugged and steep 4WD road
Hazards: Rocky, steep, dirt road with some cliff areas. Loose terrain strewn with twigs, pine cones and kiawe in the lower elevations. Hunting.
History: Old access road. Enters Department of Hawaiian Home Lands (DHHL).
Elevation Range: 3,700 to 2,600 feet

This 3.2 mile downhill is fast and furious and caution should be exercised to avoid speeds in excess of your skill level. Here, gravity is your accelerator and your brakes are your best friend.

This dirt road begins from the lush forest of the Kamakou Preserve, which borders the Moloka'i Forest Reserve. On a clear day, the panoramic views of the northeastern coast of Lana'i, some ten miles across the Kalohi Channel, are stunningly beautiful and captivating. To the east is the Ka'anapali coastline of West Maui.

The serpentine ride begins in a mixed native forest, but the landscape quickly turns from lush vegetation to a dry kiawe infested ridgeline. The road is rugged in certain areas and requires riders to slow down significantly. Be cautious of your speed and watch for steep, dangerous turns with rutted and uneven terrain. Full suspension bikes are recommended for this trail.

A maze of turn outs and other roads intersect with this road. Follow your map closely to avoid taking a wrong fork. The general rule of thumb in this area is to stay on the road most traveled. As you leave the forest, the canopy opens and offers you incredible views of southwest Moloka'i and Lana'i. You will then enter a Slash Pine

forest with pine cones the size of softballs covering the road, so be careful. At approximately 1.6 miles from the top, stay left at the first fork then right at the second and left at the third. This will lead you to a forestry gate that enters Department of Hawaiian Home Lands (DHHL). Bicycles are strictly prohibited beyond this point. From this elevation you can see many ancient fishponds on the shoreline that date back to the 1200's. Relax and enjoy the view before the ride back up.

Bike Tours - Moloka'i
Moloka'i Ranch

How to get there: From Kaunakakai, head west on Maunaloa Highway 460 until you reach the end of the state highway at the 17 mile marker. On your right you will find the Moloka'i Ranch Outfitters Center. Check in here to meet your tour guide and get outfitted with your bike and other equipment.

Moloka'i Ranch: various ride lengths (inquire within)
Rating: Beginner to advanced
Special: Multi-day adventure park. Access only permitted with over night stay.
Note: Over 100 miles of marked trail. 4WD roads and single track.
Hazards: Some loose terrain and cliff areas. Hot and sunny side of island. Bring sunscreen. Swim only in areas directed by your guide.
Amenities: Complete bike and accessory rentals. Tentalow campsites complete with private flushing toilets, solar powered ceiling fans, lighting and heated showers. Swimming, snorkeling, kayaking, surfing, beach volleyball and canoe paddling also available by request. Lunch, snacks and water also available.
History: Moloka'i Ranch has long been an advocate for land and cultural preservation while highlighting cultural diversity.
Elevation Range: 1,400 feet to sea level

Moloka'i Ranch has over 53,000 acres of property which cover most of western Moloka'i. With trail names like Ankle Biter, Blood Drive and Ditch of Doom, expect to find an epic playground of single track. Influenced by North Vancouver trials riders, sample Moloka'i Ranch's Skills Corral. Stay over night in one of the ranch's bungalow-sized tents and enjoy more than just one day of the other outdoor ranch activities, which include just about everything from horseback riding to a ropes course, to a whole sea of water sports adventures.

Mountain biking tours can be tailored to include all skill levels from basic cycling to advanced riding. Ride the green pasture lands of Na'iwa where you can gaze down steep sea cliffs and see the historical peninsula of Kalaupapa. Your friendly and knowledgeable tour guide will give you a history of the various parts of the ranch and its unique past, with nearly a hundred years as a working cattle ranch.

For added excitement, take a guided downhill night ride from the Outfitters Center to Kaupoa Beach. Shuttle vans return to the top every hour. A morning Gravity Ride starts every morning off right. Descend fast single track or dirt road to the sparkling Hawaiian waters off western Moloka'i's Kolo or Kaupoa Beaches. Inquire about the many beach activities that are offered once you get there. Nearby Hale o Lono Harbor is where sand was mined from Papohaku Beach and shipped to Waikiki. Today, the harbor is known best as the starting point for the Moloka'i to O'ahu outrigger canoe race which attracts competitive teams from as far as California and Australia. If it's outdoor fun you want, Moloka'i Ranch has it. Call today to make a reservation. Contact phone numbers are in the Appendix.

Lana'i - The Pineapple Island

Lana'i is 18 miles long and 13 miles wide and is sixth largest of the Hawaiian Islands. It has only three main roads and no traffic signals or parking meters. Since the end of pineapple production in 1994, endless acres of abandoned pineapple fields have provided plenty of red dirt roads and miles of off-road fun. Choose from a wide variety of mountain biking trails. Take a leisurely ride along the many miles of coastal roads, or challenge the arduous mountain trail over Lana'ihale, the highest peak on the island at 3,370 feet.

There are plenty of dirt roads for the beginner mountain biker. Take a ride out north to the Garden of the Gods and see the fascinating rock formations formed from many years of wind and rain erosion.

Most of Lana'i is privately owned by the Dole Company, and while visitors are welcomed, Dole asks that riders respect the natural environment and tread lightly. Ride only on designated dirt roads and wear bright colored clothing to

help ensure visibility by hunters who share the forest area.

After a hard days ride, stay the night in one of the fine luxurious resorts here. The Lodge at Ko'ele and the Manele Bay Hotel both offer visitors Hawaiian hospitality and comfortable rooms in stylish surroundings.

For the thrifty riders, camping is permitted at the historic Hulopo'e Beach Park next to the Manele Bay Hotel. Hulopo'e was once a thriving Hawaiian community dating back to 900 AD. The beach park provides showers, restrooms and picnic tables. Mingle with the dolphins and turtles while snorkeling at this beautiful beach on Lana'i's southeastern shore.

Chances are you might have arrived on Lana'i via the water shuttle from Lahaina, Maui. From Hulopo'e Beach, Manele Harbor is just a minute walk to board the Lana'i Expeditions water shuttle which will take you across the 'Au'au Channel back to Lahaina. If you need to rent a car, the only show in town is Lana'i City Service. Shuttles are available between the airport and the hotels.

Don't miss a visit to Lana'i City, a quaint old plantation town tucked away in a pine forest on the leeward side of Lana'ihale. At 1,600 feet, this small town is cool year round and everything is within walking distance.

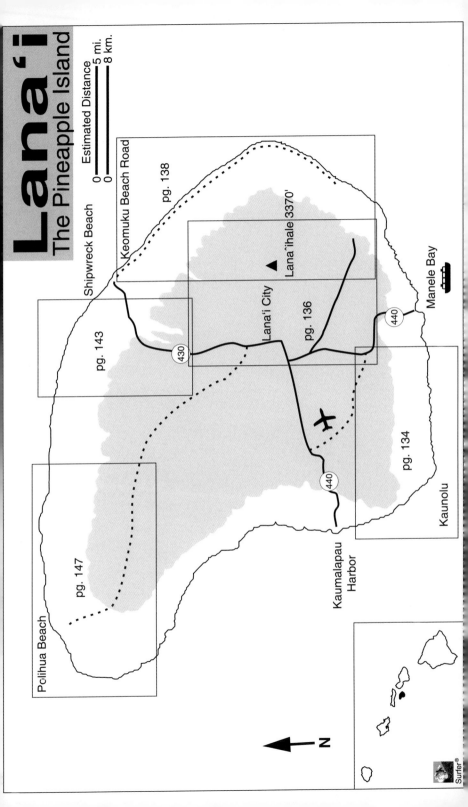

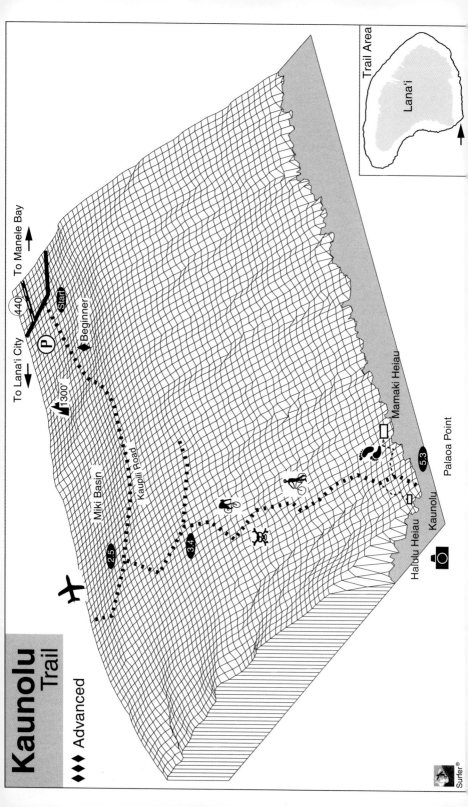

Kaunolu Trail

How to get there: From Lana'i City, turn onto Kaumalapa'u Highway 440 and left onto Manele Road 440. Proceed down and across the Palawai Basin. Just beyond the 9 mile marker, Manele Road turns left. Go straight at this intersection and veer right immediately onto the dirt road towards the southwest. Follow the road most traveled.

Kaunolu: 10.6 miles round trip
Rating: Beginner- upper road, Advanced - lower road
Special: No permit needed. Do not ride on the ancient foot trails or disturb any of the natural environment. Keep bicycles outside the interpretive park and stay on the main roads only.
Note: Rugged 4WD dirt road
Hazards: Vehicular traffic, steep rugged road with loose rocks and cliff areas. Coastal areas are hazardous during high surf. Kiawe.
Amenities: None
History: Kaunolu was an ancient ahupua'a and home of Halulu, an ancient pu'uhonua (City of Refuge). An interpretive park is located near the ocean.
Elevation Range: 1,300 feet to sea level

Begin this ride where the dirt road meets Manele Road 440. This dirt road is named Kaupili Road, but isn't marked with signs. The first 2.5 miles is ideal for beginners and offers a wide, semi-level dirt road through abandoned pineapple fields that were last harvested during 1994.

At approximately 2.5 miles, turn left towards the ocean between two posts. This marks the beginning of the rugged descent to Kaunolu. Only advanced riders should attempt this three mile downhill.

You will find many intersecting dirt roads, so stay on the road most traveled and follow the map. At 3.4 miles, the road veers to the right between another set of posts and finally reaches the ancient fishing village of Kaunolu. Vegetation is sparse, but some native Hawaiian cotton (ma'o) still grows here among the kiawe and haole koa.

At approximately 5.3 miles the road ends at Palaoa Point. This area was once a pu'uhonua (City of Refuge) known as Halulu, meaning "thundering roar". Kaunolu was a thriving Hawaiian community from 1600 to the late 1800's. Here, King Kamehameha I resided around the turn of the century. Near the coast, you will find ancient paved trails, petroglyphs, house and temple foundations. An interpretive park near the shoreline offers visitors a hiking trail with signage providing descriptions of what life in the village was like. Looking to the north from the waters edge, majestic sea cliffs stand tall and dark against the blue Pacific. During calm ocean conditions, snorkeling is excellent here.

Midday temperatures are hot on this arid coastline, so pack plenty of water and take your time on the strenuous pedal back up. Uphill may require some walking.

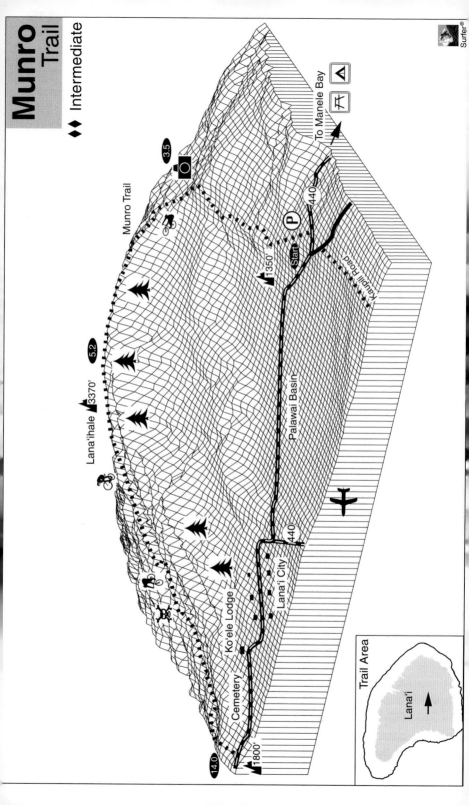

Munro Trail
◆ Intermediate

To Manele Bay

Munro Trail

3.5

5.2

Lana'ihale ▲ 3370'

1350'

Start

P

440

Kaupili Road

Palawai Basin

440

Lana'i City

Ko'ele Lodge

Cemetery

1800'

14.0

Trail Area

Lana'i

Surfer®

Munro Trail

How to get there: From Lana'i City, take Kaumalapa'u Highway 440 and turn left onto Manele Road (also 440). Proceed down and across Palawai Basin and follow the road to the left towards Manele Bay. Turn mauka onto the dirt road across from the 10 mile marker on Manele Road 440. An above ground water pipe marks the beginning of the dirt road that leads to Munro Trail.

Munro Trail: 14 miles one way
Rating: Intermediate to advanced.
Special: Private land. No permit needed.
Note: 4WD road.
Hazards: Steep road, loose terrain and cliff areas. 4WD vehicular traffic is common. Slippery when wet.
Amenities: None
History: Named after George Munro who began a reforestation project here during the 1950's. Cook Pines were planted on the summit of Lana'ihale to attract precipitation and create rain for the lower elevations. It worked.
Elevation Range: 1,350 to 3,370 feet

There are many intersecting dirt roads before reaching the one road that traverses Lana'ihale. Stay on the road most traveled.

This 4WD road traverses Lana'ihale, the highest point on the island at 3,370 feet. This hidden trail takes you from dryland forest to wetland forest via a rigorous and challenging uphill pedal to the summit. This ride is hot and offers little shade until you reach the summit area. Be prepared, carry extra water, sunscreen, hi-energy snacks and pace yourself accordingly.

Passing through miles of abandoned pineapple fields stirs memories of the former plantation days on Lana'i. Now, only hunters, hikers, bikers and visitors in their rented 4WD's roam the back hills.

Once on the ridge top, your view may include five major islands. On a clear day, Moloka'i, Maui, Kaho'olawe, Hawai'i and even O'ahu can be seen from certain sections of Lana'ihale.

A six mile downhill ride to Ko'ele offers fun and challenging turns with steep grades. The trail becomes slippery when wet, so use caution if it's raining or the road is puddled.

At approximately 10 miles, go left at the intersection to follow the road down through thick forest vegetation and tree cover. Soon you will ascend the last hill climb and pass the cemetery on your left. Go left at Keomuku Road to return to Lana'i City.

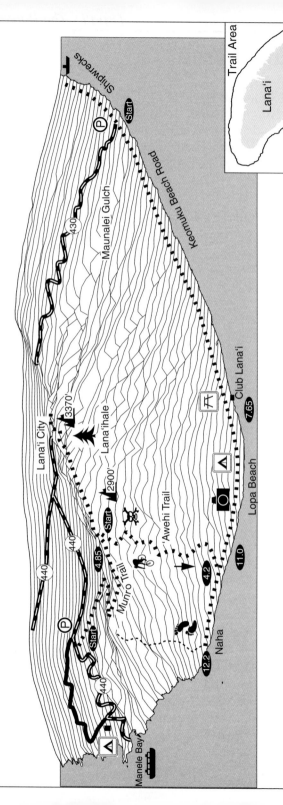

'Awehi Trail

Keomuku Beach Road

♦♦♦ Advanced

♦ Beginner

Trail Area

Lana'i

Shipwrecks

Start

P

430

Maunalei Gulch

Keomuku Beach Road

Club Lana'i

7.65

Lopa Beach

3370

Lana'i City

Lana'ihale

2900

'Awehi Trail

11.0

4.2

Start

440

4.85

Munro Trail

440

Start

P

440

12.2

Naha

Manele Bay

'Awehi Trail

How to get there: Located on the windward side of Lana'ihale, 'Awehi is accessed from the 2,900 foot level of the Munro Trail. The 'Awehi turn off is approximately 4.85 miles up Munro Trail from the 10 mile marker at Manele Road 440. A small sign indicates the 'Awehi access.

'Awehi Trail: 4.2 miles one way down
Rating: Advanced
Special: Private land. No permit is required.
Note: Rugged 4WD road. Part of loop ride. See text.
Hazards: Loose steep terrain, rocky, slippery when wet and steep cliffs. Possible 4WD vehicular traffic. Kiawe thorns.
Amenities: None
History: Old access road
Elevation Range: 2,900 feet to sea level

The 'Awehi Trail is an alternate route accessed from the Munro Trail. Much more riding is involved than just this 4.2 mile downhill. Riders use 'Awehi as a small part of a 32 mile loop that will bring them back to Lana'i City. The use of 'Awehi Trail will require riders to proceed out an 11 mile coastal dirt and sand road known as Keomuku Beach Road, and then pedal up the six mile paved Keomuku Road 430 to reach the city of Lana'i. It is a steep and rugged road that is recommended only as a downhill for the advanced cyclist.

To access 'Awehi, ride up the Munro Trail for approximately 4.85 miles, then turn right onto 'Awehi and drop down the steep and tricky 4WD road which is laced with loose rock and dirt. The view of Maui's Ka'anapali shoreline is incredible from here so don't forget to stop on occasion to check out the sights.

At the bottom of this 4.2 mile downhill, turn left onto Keomuku Beach Road. From here, it's just 3.4 miles to Club Lana'i. For a small fee, you can enjoy food and drink, participate in some fun activities and meet other visitors that have arrived by boat from Lahaina, Maui. Don't have to much fun because you still have approximately 15 miles to go to get back to Lana'i City.

Refer to the map description of Keomuku Beach Road for a list of what to expect along this coastal route. See map.

Keomuku Beach Road

How to get there: From Lana'i City, head north past The Lodge at Ko'ele and continue down Keomuku Road 430 six miles to sea level. Go straight at the dirt road and follow it to the right to access Keomuku Beach Road.

Keomuku Beach Road: 12.25 miles one way
Rating: Beginner to advanced
Special: Some residence live along this route. Stay on main road. No permit needed.
Note: 4WD road. See 'Awehi Trail for alternative access.
Hazards: Deep sand and mud in certain sections, often laced with kiawe thorns. Use caution where intermittent streams run into the ocean.
Amenities: None
History: Passes through the once thriving village of Keomuku. *Keomuku*, lit. "the shortened sand".
Elevation range: Sea level

This is Lana'i's longest coastal road, and it is usually hot and dry. Bring plenty of water and sunscreen. Kiawe trees line the entire road, so be prepared with your tire liners and patch kit. See Bicycle Maintenance for further information.

Keomuku Beach Road, a scenic dirt road that follows the eastern coastline of Lana'i, is semi-level with plenty of ruts and mud holes. It makes for a fun adventure for riders of all skill levels.

To your left, across the 'Au'au Channel lie the beaches of West Maui. Ka'anapali is easily visible with its jungle of hotels and condos that line the shore. As you continue, the road passes through one of Lana'i's historical villages, Keomuku. Near 5.75 miles is Ka Lanakila O Ka Malamalama Church. It was built in 1903 and still stands today. This landmark is the site of what was once a thriving community. Nearly 2,000 residence lived here in the late 1890's and worked in the fields of the Maunalei Sugar Company. After a few short years, this coastline proved to be unsuitable for agriculture and the community slowly dispersed.

Further along on your ride, you will pass Club Lana'i, a famous tourist retreat on the beach. Boats full of malihini's from Lahaina arrive here and participate in a wide range of activities, including kayaking and mountain biking.

Just ahead is Lopa Beach, a prime summer time surf spot for

many of the locals. The end of the road is known as Naha and is a popular spot for local fishermen. Caution is advised when swimming along this coastline. No lifeguards here and ocean conditions can be hazardous during swell activity and high winds. Enjoy your ride back!

Shipwreck Beach

How to get there: Located on the northeastern side of Lana'i, proceed to the end of Keomuku Road 430. The road ends and forks onto a dirt road. Go left and follow this sandy road to the end.

Shipwreck Beach: 3 miles round trip
Rating: Beginner to advanced
Special: Passes old fishing shacks known as Federation Camp.
Note: Dirt and sandy road.
Hazards: Vehicular traffic. May be hazardous during high surf and tides. Kiawe thorns.
Amenities: None
History: Old 1930's Federation Camp fishing huts. The exposed shipwreck has been stuck on the shallow outer reef since post World War II.
Elevation Range: Sea level

This is a short coastal ride, but be prepared for hot and arid conditions. This twisting road travels under many kiawe trees past old 1930's fishing huts known as Federation Camp. Continuing further to Kaiolohia Bay, the road ends and you'll find a couple of old picnic tables and a variety of walking paths that proceed further.

Along the coastal foot trail, explorers will catch a glimpse of a post World War II ship stuck on the reef, results from an unsuccessful attempt to sink the ship in the Kalohi Channel. This ship and and another to the north are permanently wedged on the shallow reef. Across the Kalohi Channel to the north is the island of Moloka'i.

The strong trade winds that blow from the northeast create murky and undesirable swimming conditions along this coast. On occasion, the water may become clear and glassy when the winds are light or absent. Fishing is also popular along this coast.

From the picnic tables, head south on foot to explore the many ancient Hawaiian petroglyphs that exist here. Look for the splotches of white paint along the foot path to confirm you are in the correct area. Do not disturb the old sites or any of the plantlife.

Mahana Trail
Shipwrecks

◆ Beginner

Surfer®

Lana'i

Trail Area

To Lana'i City

Kuahua Trail

P

Start

1750'

Keomuku Road

Mahana Trail

3.0

3.0

1000'

6

Maunalei Gulch

430

Lana'ihale

Start

1.5

Federation Camp

Shipwreck Beach

Mahana Trail

How to get there: Head north along Keomuku Road 430, just 2.1 miles past The Lodge at Ko'ele. Entry to Mahana Trail is on the left through the gate. Close all gates behind you.

Mahana Trail: 6 miles round trip
Rating: Beginner to advanced
Special: Cooperative Game Management Area (CGMA). Close and latch all gates behind you. Stay on main road and do not stray onto hunting trails.
Note: 4WD road. No permit needed.
Hazards: Loose and rocky terrain in some sections. Hunting and possible 4WD vehicular traffic.
Amenities: None
History: Old access road. *Mahana,* lit. "warm" or "having two branches or forks".
Elevation Range: 1,750 to 1,000 feet

Mahana Trail is an excellent beginners road with challenging hills and loose soil to pedal through. From Mahana you will have spectacular views of Moloka'i's south shore and West Maui.

The road starts off through an ironwood forest near the gated entrance and comes to a clearing with a stunning view. Stay on the road most traveled and follow your map. At .6 mile, the road forks. Kuahua Trail to the left and Mahana Trail to the right.

Kuahua Road is a long and fast downhill over a rutted out dirt road recommended for the intermediate rider. Passing the fence line bordering the Kanepu'u Preserve, Kuahua continues for approximately 3.0 miles down toward the northeastern coastline.

To follow Mahana Trail, riders must turn right at the .6 mile fork and follow the trail down. The road will fork a few more times. Stay on the road most traveled. At 1.6 miles, stay left and proceed down another 1.2 miles until the roads ends at a fence line at the 1,000 foot level. From here, riders are required to back track along the same path to return to the starting position.

If you still have the energy, proceed down the Kuahua Trail as far as your abilities permit. Fun and challenging dirt road that increases in difficulty the further down you go.

Garden of The Gods - Kanepu'u Polihua Road

How to get there: From Lana'i City, head north along Keomuku Road 430. Turn left at the tennis courts just .25 mile past The Lodge at Ko'ele. Proceed down the gravel road for .75 mile and turn right at the end onto Polihua Road.

Polihua Road: 11 miles one way to Polihua Beach
Rating: Beginner road to Garden of the Gods (GOTG).
                 Intermediate to advanced beyond GOTG
Special: No permit needed. Do not disturb wildlife or stray off the road. Hot and dry. Bring plenty of water.
Note: 4WD dirt road. Do not stray onto hunting foot paths.
Hazards: 4WD vehicles. Loose terrain and rocky surfaces. Kiawe thorns near Polihua Beach.
Amenities: None
History: Garden of the Gods is a result of years of erosion from wind and rain. Many cairns have been built here by local residents as monuments of good luck. *Polihua*, Lit. "eggs in bosom", because many green sea turtles nest along this beach.
Elevation Range: 1,740 feet to sea level at Polihua Beach

The first six miles of Polihua Road to GOTG provides an excellent adventure for beginners. The road passes through what was once one of the world's largest pineapple plantations. Several cattle grates help keep out the wild axis deer that destroy much of the fragile ecosystem. Near the five mile mark is Kanepu'u Preserve. It has been fenced in to protect the endangered plants within the preserve.

Just one mile further is Garden of the Gods. At 1,740 feet elevation, this photogenic area provides an eerie feeling of ancient times in Hawai'i. Riders will have flawless views of neighboring Moloka'i across the Kalohi Channel and on clear days, the island of O'ahu to the northwest.

Beyond GOTG, Polihua Road winds down a steep five mile declivity. On windy days, loose dirt is easily stirred up into a clouds of red dust that constantly gets into your eyes. Remember that it's a grueling five mile return trip to GOTG, so only proceed as far as you're willing to pedal back up.

If you're the die hard type, the beach at Polihua should be

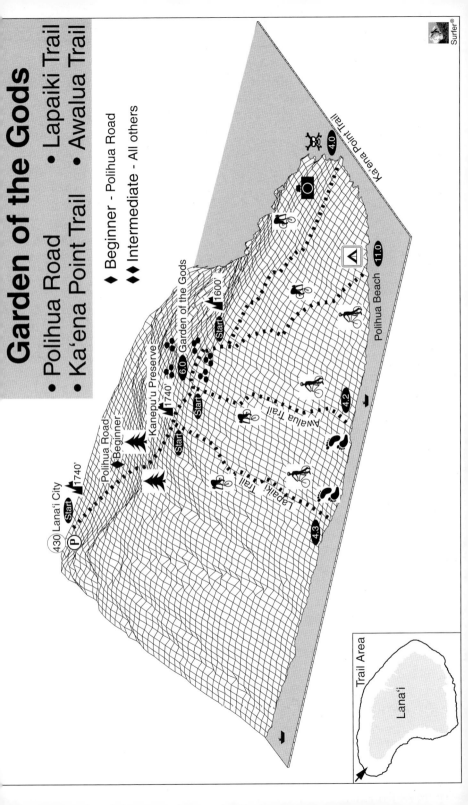

worth the ride. It's a beautiful white sand beach that runs along the north coast of Lana'i. However, due to strong and dangerous currents that usually flow westward, swimming is not recommended.

As for the beach, strong trade winds create sand storms that can be irritating and sometimes painful to the skin. After your beach experience, try to enjoy the ride back up!

View of Moloka'i from Polihua Road, Lana'i.

Lapaiki Trail

How to get there: Follow directions to Garden of the Gods on Polihua Road. Just before the GOTG, at approximately 5.2 miles, the road forks to the right and heads down Lapaiki towards the north coast of Lana'i.

Lapaiki Trail: 4.3 miles one way
Rating: Intermediate to advanced
Special: No permit needed. Stay on main road.
Note: 4WD road.
Hazards: 4WD vehicles. Rocky and loose terrain. Hunting. Kiawe. Hot and dry. Bring plenty of water. Potential ocean hazards exist on the coastline.
Amenities: None
History: *Lapaiki,* lit. "small ridge".
Elevation Range: 1,740 to sea level

Lapaiki must be accessed from Polihua Road, so riders should read Polihua and GOTG to understand the additional riding necessary.

The downhill starts off from the Garden of the Gods. The first 2 miles is flawless for downhill riding. Like many of the islands secondary roads, the terrain becomes increasingly difficult as you ascend and becomes more like a foot trail. It can be very difficult to ride, and may even be difficult to walk in certain sections. Advanced riders may find it fun and challenging, but, a novice rider may enjoy it more as a hike instead.

The trail is hot and dry, and riders are urged to carry extra water. Moloka'i and the shipwrecks along Lana'i's northeastern coast are easily seen from this section of the island. Swimming is not recommended at Lapaiki Beach because of poor conditions.

Awalua Trail

How to get there: Follow directions to Garden of the Gods on Polihua Road. Just before GOTG, the road forks to the right and heads down Awalua towards the north coast of Lana'i.

Awalua: 4.2 miles one way
Rating: Intermediate to advanced
Special: No permit needed. Stay on main road.
Note: 4WD road.
Hazards: 4WD vehicles. Rocky and loose terrain. Hunting. Kiawe thorns. Hot and dry. Bring plenty of water. Potential ocean hazards exist on the coastline.
Amenities: None
History: *Awalua*, Lit. "double harbor".
Elevation Range: 1,740 to sea level

Awalua must be accessed from Polihua Road, so riders should read Polihua and GOTG to understand the additional riding necessary.

To find Awalua, turn right at the fork just before the large stone indicating Garden of the Gods. The upper portion of the Awalua trail is a 4WD road that starts off with smooth, easy riding for the first mile, becoming gradually rougher as you descend the mountain. The terrain consists of loose rocks and kiawe thorns towards the bottom. At times, the road may become too difficult to negotiate and riders may have to dismount and walk their bikes.

Enjoyable views are found along this ride, including the abandoned shipwrecks resting on the outer reef. The beach at Awalua is commonly windy and the water murky. Swimming is not recommended. The ride back up is hot and slow going, so pace yourself and drink plenty of water.

Ka'ena Point

How to get there: Follow directions to Polihua Road and Garden of the Gods. Approximately 1.25 miles beyond the GOTG, turn left to Ka'ena.

Ka'ena Trail: 4 miles one way down
Rating: Intermediate to advanced
Special: No permit needed. Stay on main road.
Note: 4WD road.
Hazards: 4WD vehicles. Rocky and loose terrain. Hunting. Kiawe. Hot and dry. Bring plenty of water. Steep cliffs and potential ocean hazards at the end.
Amenities: None
History: Ka'ena was known to be a place of exile for female convicts in 1837.
Elevation Range: 1,600 feet to sea level

Ka'ena must be accessed from Polihua Road, so riders should read Polihua and GOTG to understand the additional riding necessary.

This difficult downhill 4WD road leads to the blue ocean of Lana'i's northwest coastline. The area is lined with steep and rugged cliffs that battle the rough ocean swells year 'round. During the calmer summer months, fishing, snorkeling or swimming can be enjoyed by people with knowledge and experience in the ocean.

During your descent, many rutted out areas of the road require skill to negotiate. The uphill is slow going and may require some walking. A variety of short dirt roads intersect Ka'ena and head north and south. Follow the main road and use your map to avoid confusing forks.

Bike Tours - Lana'i

Adventure Lana'i Eco-Center offers downhill / coastal bike tours and off-road mountain bike treks throughout the diverse terrain of Lana'i. The trips are tailored for beginner through intermediate bikers. All bike treks begin with instruction on basic mountain biking techniques, equipment, and safety. All of the Adventure Lana'i Eco-Center mountain bike treks include van support.

Choose the Keomuku/Petroglyphs Downhill Bike Trek and enjoy an exhilarating downhill bike tour down Keomuku Road towards Shipwreck Beach. Then take a short hike to explore the Po'aiwa Gulch and see ancient petroglyphs.

Another tour conquers the Munro Trail over the 3,370 foot Lana'ihale. Ferns and tropical plants cover the steep gorges on each side of the narrow ridge.

The Garden of the Gods adventure leads you through fields where pineapples were once harvested. As you enter the unearthly Garden of the Gods, the terrain changes dramatically. Years of erosion have left pinnacles of rocks, large boulders, and bizarre rock formations scattered throughout the rainbow-stained landscape. Contact numbers are listed in the Appendix.

After a hard ride, riders relax at the Lana'i City Pineapple Festival.

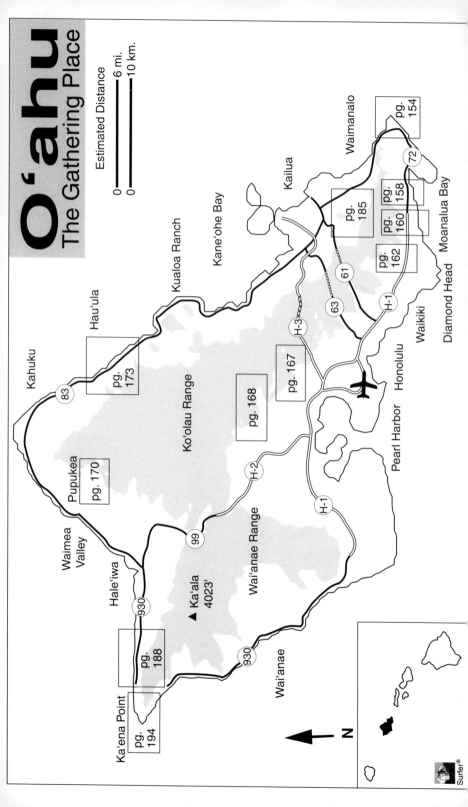

O'ahu - The Gathering Place

O'ahu is the third largest of the Hawaiian Islands and is home to more than 850,000 residents. It is 44 miles across and 30 miles wide with 112 miles of coastline. Honolulu, the state capital, is surrounded by the Ko'olau and Wai'anae Mountain Ranges. The highest peak on the island is Ka'ala in the Wai'anae Range, which stands at 4,023 feet. Bicycles are prohibited on Ka'ala, however, incredible biking trails are found on the north end of the Wai'anae Range and on many ridges and valleys of the Ko'olau Range. Compared to the neighboring islands, O'ahu has the most single track open to mountain bikes.

Riders of all skill levels will find a myriad of trails and dirt roads to explore on O'ahu. Coastal trips with incredible scenic back drops offer fulfilling off-road adventures along some of the most pristine coastline in the world. Being the most populated island, riders should expect to see other trail users on most any trail.

After mountain biking through miles of lush green valleys and ridgelines, visitors with a thirst for night life can find just about everything under the sun in world famous Waikiki. Day time beach dwellers can enjoy countless hours of surfing, sailing and canoe rides in the waves off the shores of Waikiki. Don't miss the world class surfing on the North Shore at Waimea Bay, Pipeline, and Sunset Beach.

For further information on O'ahu's activities and places of interest, contact the Hawai'i Visitors and Convention Bureau. Their phone number is available in the Appendix.

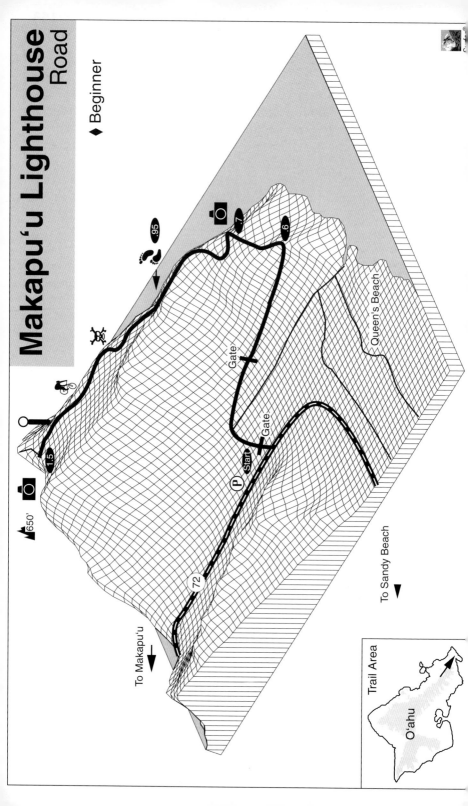

Makapu'u Lighthouse Road

How to get there: Located at the easternmost tip of O'ahu's Ko'olau Range. Follow Kalaniana'ole Highway 72 east-bound approximately two miles past Sandy Beach Park. Paved access begins between Hawai'i Kai Golf Course and Makapu'u Lookout. Park off the highway and do not leave valuables in car. Carry your bike around the locked gate and proceed up the paved road.

Makapu'u Lighthouse Road: 3.0 miles round trip
Rating: Beginner to advanced
Special: Permit not needed.
Note: Paved road only. Wet ride ok.
Hazards: Unkept paved road. Deep cracks, potholes, loose gravel and cliffs.
Amenities: None
History: Now automated, lighthouse used to be manned. *Makapu'u*, lit. "bulging eye" or "hill beginning".
Elevation Range: 100 to 650 feet

This is a scenic uphill ride to the Makapu'u Lighthouse viewpoint. You will most likely encounter other bikers and hikers, so be prepared to slow or stop, especially on the downhill run. Beautiful scenic views are found on the entire length of the road. The dry coastal environment is home for cactus, kiawe and haole koa trees. The first viewpoint is just beyond the second gate at about the .6 mile mark. (see map) Below to your right is the Queen's Beach area. From this elevated view, many dirt roads and trails can be seen. Down the coast about two miles is Sandy Beach Park, one of the best sites for bodysurfing, bodyboarding and skimboarding.

At the .7 mile mark, you will be able to look out over the Ka'iwi or Moloka'i Channel. The islands of Moloka'i and Lana'i are usually visible. On a clear day, Maui's Haleakala "house of the sun" can be seen hiding behind the eastern tip of Moloka'i. Between the months of November and May, you might see some passing humpback whales breaching in the blue Pacific. On occasion, seabirds like albatross', frigates and boobies fly by in search of the day's fresh catch

Proceed further up past two hairpin turns and you will come to a white concrete block on the right. On your left is a great view of two dormant volcanos. The closer one is Koko Crater. Off in the distance is Leʻahi or Diamond Head which sits next to Waikiki. On the right side of the road, you'll see a small painted arrow which points down the cliff. This marks a trail head, but is for hikers only. Do not attempt the trail on a bike. It ascends a steep cliff comprised of loose rocks and gravel to a cluster of blow holes and small tide pools at sea level. This area is very hazardous during big surf, so stay clear during high surf episodes.

Proceeding further, the paved road splits off to the right (approx. 1.2 mile mark). This is a closed entrance to the lighthouse. Only Coast Guard personnel are allowed beyond the locked gate.

The top of the road is the end of this short ride. Two platforms with hand rails have been constructed for safe viewing of the jagged sea cliffs below. The higher platform has the best view of the historic Makapuʻu Lighthouse below to the right. Two islands are visible below. The smaller is Kaohikaipu or Black Rock and the larger is Manana Island or Rabbit Island. Both of them are state bird refuges. Makapuʻu Beach and Sea Life Park are below to the left. Standing here, you can see the shoreline from Waimanalo to Kaʻaʻawa and the Mokulua Islands off of Kailua. The prominent three pointed peak in the distance is Olomana which is the finish point of the Maunawili Trail.

View from Makapuʻu Lighthouse Road.

Kuli'ou'ou Trails

How to get there: Located on southeastern O'ahu, Kuli'ou'ou lies between Hawai'i Kai and Niu Valley. Traveling on Kalaniana'ole Highway 72 , turn mauka on Kuli'ou'ou Road and proceed about a mile into the valley. Turn right on Kala'au Place and park at the end of the road. Pass the cable and go right at the fork. Continue past the hiker check-in station to access both trails.

Kuli'ou'ou Valley Trail: 1.5 miles round trip
Rating: Intermediate to advanced
Special: No permit needed. Stay on main trail.
Note: Single track. DO NOT ride when wet or raining.
Hazards: Cliffs, loose terrain, flooding and hunters in valley.
Amenities: None
History: *Kuli'ou'ou*, lit. "sounding knee" referring to a knee drum called punui.
Elevation Range: 230 to 500 feet

This is a short trail which follows the valley floor along the right side of the stream bed. Slightly bumpy and off camber terrain with an abundance of roots and rocks. Use caution if you get caught in the rain as this trail is slippery when wet. When you reach the .75 mile mark, a footpath proceeds through very rocky terrain. The valley becomes quite lush with a variety of ferns, kukui, mango and guava trees. For bird watchers, the valley is full of song by our fine feathered friends.

Kuli'ou'ou Ridge Trail: 3.0 miles round-trip
Rating: Advanced
Special: No permit needed. Stay on main trail.
Note: Single track. DO NOT ride when wet or raining.
Hazards: Cliffs, roots, rocks, loose terrain and hunters in valley.
Amenities: Picnic table with shelter at top of single track.
History: Trail was cut in 1990.
Elevation Range: 230 to 1,100 feet

The valley trail intersects the ridge trail near the .3 mile mark. From here, turn right and follow this challenging ride that zigzags up the right side of the valley. Cliffs exist along most of the trail, so use caution. Some difficult areas with roots and rocks are found in various spots along this winding trail. The hairpin turns and drop-off sections can be trying for anyone, even with years of experience.

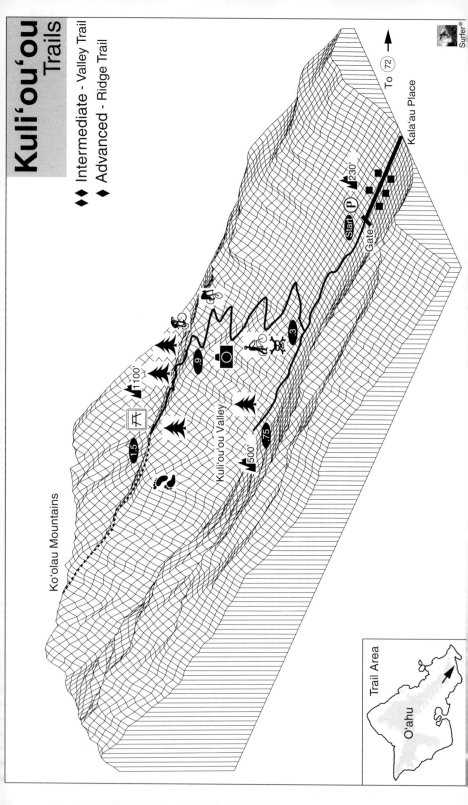

There are a few sections which will require dismounting, but most of the trail is ridable and fun.

The trail passes through a Norfolk pine forest and ends up at a shelter with two picnic tables near 1,100 feet. There is a cleared section of red dirt that's good for messing around and practicing your trials techniques.

The trail continues past the shelter for a short distance before turning into an arduous foot trail. The trail ascends the final peak to the summit where the view of Waimanalo is well worth the hike. No bikes allowed on summit trail. The downhill is a blast, but as always, watch for hikers.

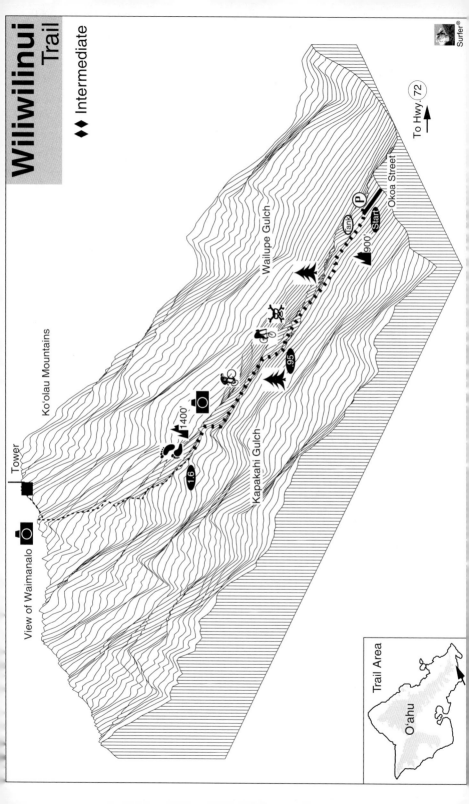

Wiliwilinui Trail

How to get there: Located above Wai'alae Iki on O'ahu's south shore. Turn mauka off Kalaniana'ole Highway 72 and head up Laukahi Street. Approximately 1.6 miles up, you will come to a guard shack where you will get your day pass. Continue up Laukahi to the end and turn left on Okoa Street. Proceed to the end of the paved road and park. Be sure to observe signs and parking restrictions. Keep your day pass on the driver's side of your dashboard. The cable across the road marks the beginning of the Wiliwilinui Ridge Trail.

Wiliwilinui Ridge Trail: 3.2 miles round trip
Rating: Intermediate to advanced
Special: No permit needed. A day pass from the guard shack on Laukahi Street is necessary. Bike rack available at summit trail.
Note: 4WD dirt road. Wet ride ok. No bikes on summit trail.
Hazards: Cliffs, possible 4WD's, loose terrain, slippery when wet.
Amenities: Parking
History: *Wiliwilinui*, lit. "large wiliwili", as that of the native tree.
Elevation Range: 900 to 1,400 feet

The Ko'olau Range offers many valleys and ridges to explore. This special bike trek is a must for mountain biking enthusiasts. The first 1.6 miles of this trail is a 4WD road and is plenty wide for mountain bikes to ride side by side. A variety of steep uphills and downhills along with some rutted out areas make for an exciting ride. Mud puddles are common along this road and may be deeper than they appear. Seasonal strawberry guavas are found along the road side to nibble on. As you near the end of the road, watch for some fantastic valley views.

At the end of the road, a foot trail marks the final climb to the summit. No bikes are allowed on the summit trail. A bike rack is provided if you decide to lock your bike and continue on foot. From here, a one hour hike will bring you to the Wiliwilinui communications repeater on the ridge top. On a clear day, you will have an excellent view of Waimanalo and Olomana on the windward side. Looking back at the leeward side, you will catch a spectacular view from Hawai'i Kai to Makakilo. Always remember to stay on the main trail and don't attempt to get too close to cliff areas. The ground is moist and slippery and is dangerous near steep sections.

Your return trip will go by much quicker. Be careful on the hike down and don't take chances. Once you've reached your bike, a quick brake check would be appropriate before the downhill. Some short pedaling will be necessary but, fear not, the downhill sections are exhilarating and fast. Use caution near the rutted out areas and puddles. Watch for hikers around blind curves.

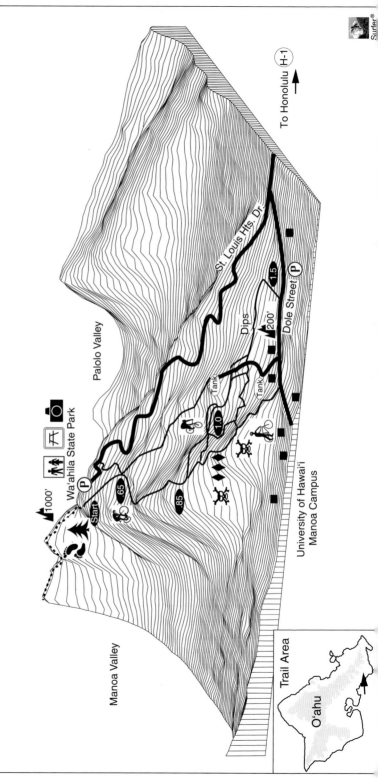

Wa'ahila Valley Trails

How to get there: Located above Kaimuki on O'ahu's south shore. From Wai'alae Avenue, turn mauka onto St. Louis Heights Drive. Follow road to the top and turn right onto Peter Street and left onto Ruth Place. Pass the gated entrance to Wa'ahila State Park. Gate is open from 7am to 7:30pm. If you're planning on staying after the park is closed, park your car outside the gate. The Wa'ahila Valley Trails will lead you to Dole Street at the bottom of St. Louis Heights. If you parked at the top parking lot, you will need to pedal back up via St. Louis Heights Drive or catch the city bus that offers a free front loading carrier for a maximum of two bikes.

Wa'ahila Valley Trails: 1.5 miles one way
Rating: Intermediate to advanced
Special: Ride as downhill ONLY. Stay on main trails.
Note: Single track with some 4WD road. DO NOT ride when wet or raining.
Hazards: Cliffs, tree stumps, loose terrain, roots and rocks.
Amenities: Parking, shelter, tables, water and restrooms.
History: The Norfolk Pine forest is the result of a former reforestation project to replace the ridge top vegetation destroyed by feral cattle in the early 1900's. The park was the site of the downhill course for the Grundig/UCI World Cup of mountain biking in 1996.
Elevation Range: 200 to 1,000 feet

A downhill mountain bikers dream trail. This is a short and challenging trail ride which winds down the ridge from the Norfolk Pine forest in Wa'ahila State Park and ends on Dole Street. Excellent views of Manoa Valley are common in the park and along the trail. The first half mile is a dirt road that is loaded with roots and small drop-offs. The trail then becomes a single track, winding in and out of guava trees, eventually coming to a fork at a telephone pole.

The upper left trail will lead you back up to the park entrance.

By going straight at the telephone pole, you will ride down through a haole koa forest with some technical rocky sections and loose terrain. This is the easier way down to Dole Street.

The hardier way is to go right at the telephone pole and follow the downhill course used during the Grundig World Cup. At the .85 mile mark, the trail splits off to the left through the dry haole koa forest. At 1.0 mile, the trail splits again. Go right for a steep drop-in known as "Buzz's Bailout" or stay left to intersect halfway down the

drop-in. Dismount and walk your bike here, if this exceeds your skill level. Following the trail out, you will cross over the cement road and continue the trail down the other side, eventually ending up on Dole Street at telephone pole #68.

The even more advanced and technical option is to stay right at the .85 mile mark and take the next left fork to a trail known as "Burms" or the following left fork known as "Technos". These names spell out the ideal terrain for downhill mountain biking. Along the trail are beautiful views of Waikiki and Diamond Head. Some thorny trees with yellow flowers are found along this path, so use care when passing them. A quarter mile further, you'll come upon some advanced technical riding over and around a section of black rocks. Some drop-offs range from 2 feet with hidden rocks in the tall grass, so use caution and tighten up your helmet. Dismount when appropriate. To exit, you will cross over the paved road and enter another rugged trail that terminates at Dole Street.

Wa'ahila Ridge Trail: .35 miles one way
Rating: Intermediate to advanced
Special: No permit needed.
Note: 4WD road. Foot trail only beyond the .35 mile mark.
Hazards: Cliffs, steep and loose terrain.
Amenities: Parking, water, shelter, tables, restrooms.
Elevation Range: 1,000 to 1,300 feet

The Wa'ahila Ridge Trail is only ridable above the State Park up to the .35 mile mark. Expect to see hikers with small children. For bikers, it's a short uphill ride which passes through a forest of Norfolk Pine and strawberry guava trees. This short uphill ride ends at a nice spot under some ironwood trees near the power lines. From here, the trail descends a steep ridge and is for hikers only.

Returning to the park and connecting with the valley trails makes this uphill ride worth the extra effort.

Tantalus Trail System

Endangered Trails: The Tantalus Trail System is considered to be endangered. It is extremely fragile due to its moist environment and overuse. The State Department of Land and Natural Resources, Division of Forestry and Wildlife has introduced a "rest period" for the Tantalus area. In early 1996, they put up signs prohibiting bicycles on this trail system. Plans to reopen select trails in this area are being negotiated.

The Tantalus Trail System consists of 14 different trails which includes the Arboretum Trail, Kanealole Trail, Maunalaha Trail, Nahuina Trail, Makiki Valley Trail, 'Ualaka'a Trail, Moleka Trail, Manoa Cliff Trail, Pu'u 'Ohi'a Trail, Pauoa Flats Trail, Nu'uanu Trail, Judd Trail, 'Aihualama Trail and Manoa Falls Trail.

Restrictions for this area are subject to change. Both kama'aina's and malihini's can make a difference by joining the many volunteer bikers and hikers to help restore and improve these trails. Inquire with DLNR - Na Ala Hele for up-to-date information. See Permit Information for contact number and read the chapter on Getting Involved in Trail Maintenance.

'Aiea Loop Trail

How to get there: Located above the town of 'Aiea. From Honolulu, take H-1 'ewa (west) bound and get off at exit 13A. Follow Moanalua Road and turn right at 'Aiea Shopping Center. Follow 'Aiea Heights Drive past the gated entrance to Kea'iwa Heiau State Recreational Park. The upper trail head starts to the right, just left of the restrooms in the park at the crest of the hill.

'Aiea Loop Trail: 4.5 miles one way loop
Rating: Intermediate to advanced
Special: No permit needed. Gate to park is open 7am-6:45pm/7am-7:45pm summer
Note: Single track. DO NOT ride if wet or raining.
Hazards: Cliffs, drop-offs, loose terrain, roots, rocks and hunters.
Amenities: Camping sites by permit only, parking, drinking water, restrooms, shelter and picnic tables.
History: Crash site of C-47 along trail. Kea'iwa Heiau is believed to be the ruins of an old medical healing site. Norfolk Pine forest planted in 1928 by Thomas McGuire. *Kea'iwa*, lit. "the mystery".
Elevation Range: 930 to 1,540 feet

'Aiea Loop Trail is one of the most fun rides in central O'ahu. Although rated as an intermediate trail, there are many technical areas where you will need to dismount. Starting from the upper end (see map), you will drop into a small gully and climb the other side over a root bound technical uphill. The trail zigzags through some well shaded vegetation and ascends the ridge top.

Just before you begin the downhill at the 1.6 mile mark, the trail on your left begins the "hike only" ridge trail to the summit. A great rest stop to take in the view before descending the opposite ridge to the park.

This downhill has some dangerous cliff areas so be extremely careful. On the valley floor to your left lies the new H-3 freeway that connects the windward and leeward sides of the island.

On your right, at approximately 2.4 miles, you will encounter several pieces of an airplane. According to historians, these are the 1943 remnants of a military C-47 cargo plane which crashed shortly after take off. It was empty and all three crew members survived the frightening crash. It was enroute to Bellows AFS from Wheeler AFB.

Continuing down the switchback, you will finally reach the valley floor and stream crossing. Dismount and carry your bike across to ensure safety. A short uphill will return you to the lower trail head at the park. Follow the paved road up approximately .25 mile to your original starting position.

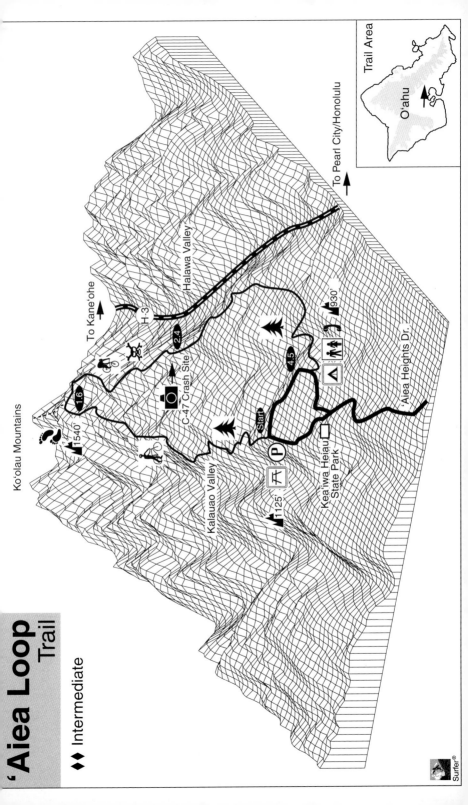

'Aiea Loop Trail

◆ Intermediate

Trail Area

O'ahu

To Pearl City/Honolulu

Ko'olau Mountains

To Kane'ohe

H-3

Halawa Valley

1540'

1.6

2.4

C-47 Crash Site

Kalauao Valley

4.5

Start

1125'

930'

Kea'iwa Heiau State Park

'Aiea Heights Dr.

Surfer®

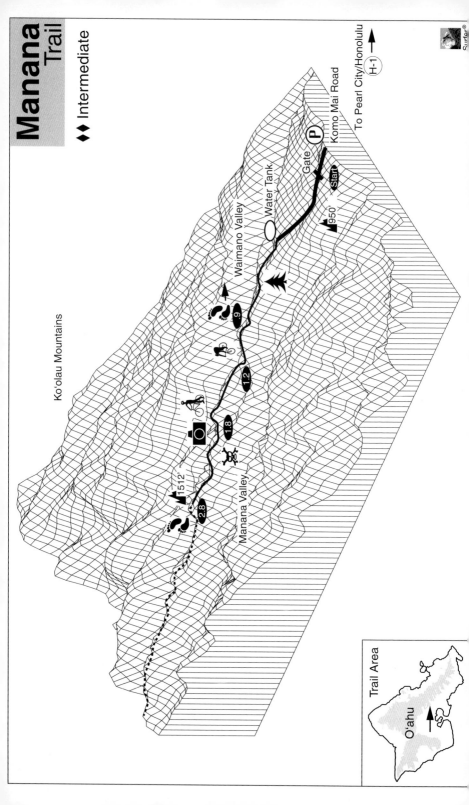

Manana Trail

How to get there: Located in Pacific Palisades, central O'ahu.
Heading north on H-1 freeway, take exit 10 Waimalu. Stay to the right and merge onto Moanalua Road. Proceed to the end and turn right at Waimano Home Road. Make a left at Komo Mai Road and follow to the end and park. Pass the locked gate and follow paved road to dirt trail head.

Manana Trail: 5.6 miles round trip
Rating: Intermediate to advanced
Special: No permit needed. Stay on main trail.
Note: Single track. DO NOT ride if wet or raining.
Hazards: Cliffs, hunters, loose terrain, roots and rocks.
Amenities: Parking
Elevation Range: 950 to 1,512 feet

An exceptional ride. The first .35 mile is a paved road. Just beyond the paved section, a beautiful single track continues up the ridge line. At approximately the .9 mile mark, the trail veers to the right, taking you to the beginning of a "hike only" trail that drops into Waimano Valley. Two beautiful pools with waterfalls lie at the bottom of the trail. Hike here another day when you aren't riding bikes.

Further up the ridge line at approximately 1.28 miles, the trail veers to the left and brings you out into the opening of another ridge. The first section is red dirt and is completely exposed. Ride further until you reach a steep cliff with a great view of Manana Valley. This is a perfect scenic overlook to break for lunch. On a clear day, the summits of the Ko'olau Range and the neighboring Wai'anae Range show their multi-shades of green and steep cliffs. Both are beautiful, yet rugged.

Dropping into the trail again will lead you to some tricky sections that will require dismounts. The trail continues only a short distance before becoming a steep incline for hiking only. The return downhill will lighten up your day with spectacular views and perfect single track. Use caution riding through the blind turns and be courteous to other trail users.

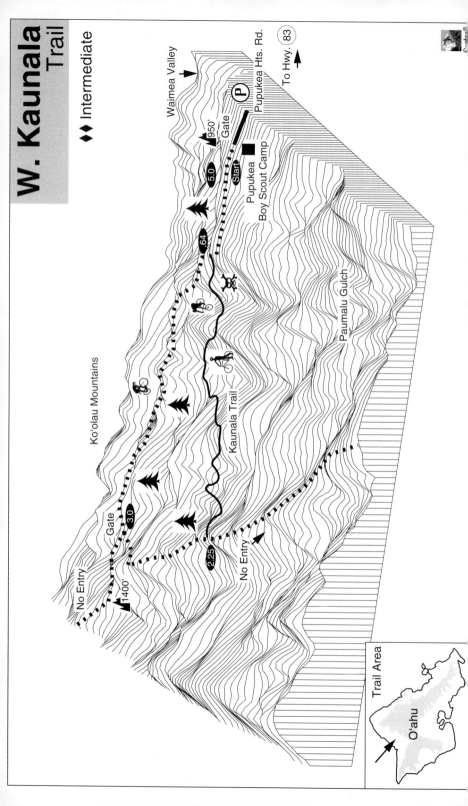

West Kaunala Trail

How to get there: Drive to the North Shore on Kamehameha Highway 83. Turn mauka on Pupukea Road which is directly across from the Sunset Fire Station. Continue up approximately 2.7 miles until you reach the end of the road and park on the public road outside the Boy Scout Camp. Ride your bike up past the locked Forest Reserve gate and follow the 4WD road approximately .64 mile until you see the Kaunala Trail head on your left.

West Kaunala Trail: 2.25 miles one way
Rating: Intermediate to advanced
Special: No permit is needed. However, access to this trail is allowed only on weekends, state and national holidays. The state shares access with the military. On weekdays, this road may be in use for military training exercises.
Note: Single track and 4WD road. On rainy days, only the access roads should be ridden. DO NOT ride single track when wet or raining. Stay on main trail.
Hazards: Cliffs, roots, rocks, recreational vehicles and hunting.
Amenities: None
History: *Kaunala*, lit. "the plaiting". Known to many local riders as the *Cambodia Trail*.
Elevation Range: 950 to 1,400 feet

This awesome trail is the epitome of tropical mountain biking. Follow the dirt road which leads you to the beginning of the single track at the .6 mile mark. Stay to the left of the sign indicating Kaunala Trail. This serpentine trail climbs a short curve and then

goes down through forests of paper bark trees.

Kaunala has an abundance of protruding roots that range from two inches to one foot in height, making it a bit more technical than the average trail. Kaunala also has downhills which will put your okole (butt) over your rear tire and uphills that will burn your legs. With all the surrounding beauty and tropical splendor, try to stay focused on the trail. There are many steep and hazardous cliff areas throughout this trail. You will see a few small foot trails that go off from the main trail. Some of these are used by hunters and should not be attempted on bike.

You will cross at least three flowing streams and traverse many ridges with thick vegetation before reaching the final climb. On your final ascent in "granny gear", you will connect to a 4WD road. Turn right and pedal up for approximately .75 mile before connecting to another dirt road. Going right will lead you two miles back to the starting point.

You may see motorcycles and 4WD trucks along this dirt road, so use caution. If you hear motorized vehicles approaching, quickly pull to the side of the road and wait until they pass. The roundtrip is approximately 5 miles.

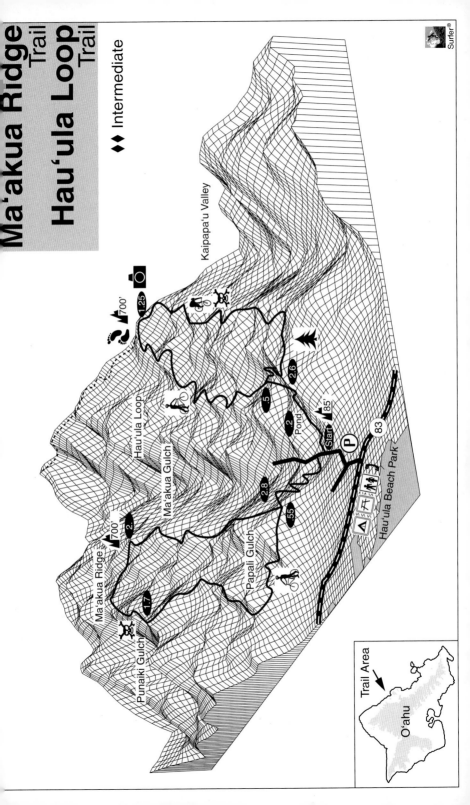

Hau'ula Loop Trail

How to get there: Located above Hau'ula Homesteads on O'ahu's northeast shore. Follow Kamehameha Highway 83 north past Sacred Falls State Park. Take a left at Hau'ula Homestead Road. When you reach the fork, turn right onto Ma'akua Road. Drive to the end of road and park. Follow the dirt road to the left. Access to the trail head will be on your right.

Hau'ula Loop: 3.0 miles round trip
Rating: Intermediate to advanced
Special: No permit needed. Stay on main trail.
Note: Single track. DO NOT ride when wet or raining.
Hazards: Loose terrain, cliffs, roots, rocks and hunting.
Amenities: Camping by permit only.
History: The Hau'ula Loop trail was cut in 1878. *Hau'ula*, lit. "red hau tree".
Elevation Range: 85 to 700 feet

Hau'ula Loop is an epic single track that zigzags up the right side of the mountain. It crosses over Waipilopilo Gulch and crests the ridge top overlooking beautiful Kaipapa'u Valley. Hau'ula Loop is a great ride without a lot of bike-carrying. The terrain consists of roots, rocks, a couple of small streams and one pond at the end of your downhill (see map). There are a couple of areas where you may need to dismount. Off-camber and rutted trail sections may be tricky. Use your own judgement and common sense.

A variety of seasonal tropical fruits, such as lilikoi (passion fruit), strawberry guava and guava are found in abundance here. Fantastic views and a flawless downhill single track makes Hau'ula Loop Trail an island treat. Bring a camera and capture your journey on film. The contrast of blue ocean against the dark green mountains make for exceptional photos.

If you still have the energy after the Hau'ula Loop Trail, try the neighboring Ma'akua Ridge Trail. When riding these two trails back to back, you will have spent the day experiencing some of the island's greatest single track.

Ma'akua Ridge Trail

How to get there: Located above Hau'ula Homesteads on O'ahu's northeast shore. Follow Kamehameha Highway 83 north past Sacred Falls State Park. Take a left at Hau'ula Homestead Road. When you reach the fork, turn right onto Ma'akua Road. Drive to end of road and park. Follow the dirt road to the left. Access to the trail head will be on the left just past the Hau'ula Loop Trail.

Ma'akua Ridge Trail: 3.35 miles round-trip
Rating: Intermediate to advanced
Special: No permit needed. Stay on main trail.
Note: Single track. DO NOT ride when wet or raining.
Hazards: Cliffs, narrow and loose terrain, roots, rocks and hunters.
Amenities: None
Elevation Range: 85 to 700 feet

You will need to carry your bike across a stream bed to reach the other side to begin this trail. This challenging uphill ride begins with a switchback up the left side of Ma'akua Gulch. Some tricky areas are found in various spots along the winding turns. Dismount where appropriate.

This loop trail will bring you back to your original starting position. You will find spectacular views of the northeastern coastline along this trail. An arduous uphill climb traverses the Papali and Punaiki Gulch. This tropical mountain side also has lilikoi and guava fruit which flourish at different times of the year. Endulging in fresh, hand-picked fruit while mountain biking on this Hawaiian trail brings a feeling of tropical paradise.

Once you've reached the final ridge top, you will find the view of Ma'akua Valley outstanding. Below, the valley whispers. The sound of leaves and branches rustling in the wind, as birds of different color navigate the steep hillside. Truly a wonder of O'ahu, Ma'akua is a must for mountain biking.

Now, get ready for a fun single track downhill. Hikers, cliff areas and some technical areas exist along this narrow trail, so use caution. The trail will connect with itself. At this intersection, hang a left and descend the same switchback to the valley floor. Be careful crossing the stream bed if the water levels are high.

Maunawili Trail

How to get there: Located on Oʻahu's windward side. From Honolulu, take the Pali Highway 61 through the Pali tunnels. Stay in your right lane and pull off at the first scenic lookout located between the 6 and 7 mile marker. Park and lock your car. The trail head is located near the scenic lookout entrance.

You may also connect to this trail from the Pali Lookout. Park your car at the lookout and follow the old Pali Road for approximately one mile to the right from viewpoint. (see map)

Maunawili Trail: 10 miles one way
Rating: Intermediate to advanced
Special: No permit needed. Stay on main trail. Long distance.
Note: Single track. DO NOT ride if wet or raining.
Hazards: Cliffs, steep grades, loose terrain, roots and rocks. During windy days, the Pali Lookout area sometimes has thousands of bees clinging to the ground for safety. The intersection of the old Pali Highway Access Trail and the Maunawili Trail has an active beehive.
Amenities: Parking
History: Single track cut in 1991 by volunteers and the Sierra Club. Also known as Maunawili Demonstration Trail. The old Pali Highway was built in 1897 and was used by windward and lee-

Maunawili Trail, O'ahu

"Go Big", O'ahu   photo: Jeff Cox Freezeaction.com

The scenic Hauʻula Loop Trail.

Hawaiʻi's largest mountain bike competition. photo: Twain Newhart

Scenic trails abound on O'ahu.

"Daily fix of adrenalin". O'ahu. photo: Jeff Cox Freezeaction.com

Bike Hawaii Tour at Ka'a'awa, O'ahu.

Kuli'ou'ou Ridge Trail, O'ahu

Volcanic ash beds, O'ahu

Wiliwilinui Ridge Trail, O'ahu

Avoiding the drop at Kuli'ou'ou.

24Hours, O'ahu. Jeff Cox Freezeaction.com

View of Dillingham Airfield from the Kealia Trail, O'ahu.

Pedaling up Mokule'ia Access Rd.

Eucalyptus trees at 'Aiea Loop Trail.

View of the Makua coast from Ka'ena Point.

Hugging the edge at ʻAiea Loop Trail.

Bike Hawaiʻi's - Oʻahu Bike & Hike Tour

It's all downhill from here! Wa'ahila Trail, O'ahu.

Night riding Wa'ahila.

Maunawili Trail, O'ahu.

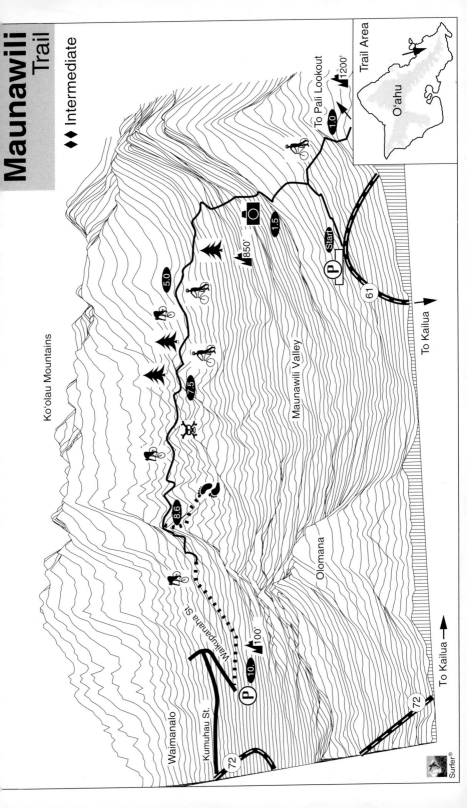

Maunawili Trail

Trail

◆ Intermediate

Ko'olau Mountains

To Palii Lookout

▲1200'

▲1.0

Trail Area

O'ahu

850'

5.0

1.5

7.5

8.6

Start

P

61

Maunawili Valley

To Kailua

Olomana

Waikupanaha St.

100'

10

P

Kumuhau St.

Waimanalo

72

72

To Kailua

72

Surfer®

ward O'ahu residents as the fastest method of crossing the Ko'olau Mountains. *Maunawili*, lit. "twisted mountain".

Elevation Range: 1,200 to 100 feet

An exceptional ride. One of O'ahu's newest trails, Maunawili Trail is already on the verge of being endangered. Often moist, this tropical environment has plenty of overgrown trees which shade the trail and prevent water evaporation. Until reconstruction of these wet areas is finished, riders should avoid all puddled areas by dismounting and walking their bikes.

Situated at the base of the Ko'olau Range, this trail offers the most scenic ride on the island. Winding in and out of numerous little valleys gives you an example of the islands volcanic makeup. As you ride, a variety of sites, sounds, terrains and landscapes make you realize why this trail is so popular with hikers and bikers. The mauka side of the trail harbors steep, intense Pali's (cliffs) and the makai side offers views of Kailua, Olomana and Waimanalo. The blue Pacific is also easy to see in the distance.

Along this 10 mile trail, you will notice a variety of trail restoration efforts made by various volunteer groups and Na Ala Hele. Water-bars, log steps and boardwalks have been constructed to help minimize impact to the soft and moist trail below. Throughout the trail, many puddled areas are found. Riders should dismount and walk your bike when passing these fragile sections of trail.

This is an out and back trail. Starting the Maunawili Trail at the Pali Highway and ending in Waimanalo, round trip totals 20 miles. Be prepared for a few hours on the trail. If you don't have a car waiting for you at the Waimanalo end, remember, it's a very long trip, so bring plenty of snacks and water. Don't forget to bring your camera.

Kuaokala Forest Reserve:

Kuaokala Access Road

How to get there: Located at the western tip of O'ahu's Wai'anae Range. Follow Farrington Highway 930 westbound past Wai'anae until you reach Keawa'ula or Yokohama Beach. Turn right and follow the Ka'ena Point Satellite Tracking Station (KPSTS) access road. You are required to stop at the guard shack to furnish a valid I.D. and a permit issued from DLNR. See Permit Information.

Kuaokala Access Road: 7.3 miles one way to Mokule'ia Access Rd.
Rating: Beginner to advanced
Special: A permit is needed to enter and exit via the KPSTS or when camping at Peacock Flats campground. See Permit Information.
Note: First 2.5 miles is paved. Then 7.3 miles of 4WD road. Wet riding ok.
Hazards: 4WD's, hunters, cliff areas. Road is slippery when wet.
Amenities: Parking, camping, portable rest room and shelter at Peacock Flats.
History: *Kuaokala*, lit. "back of the sun".
Elevation Range: 1,700 to 1,200 feet

The Kuaokala Forest Reserve offers great biking for all riding abilities. Riders can park their car at the parking area just before dropping down the hill from B Road. (See map)

For experienced riders, the roads offer a challenging complex of detours, short cuts and alternate routes. Go fast, ride hard, and enjoy the mountain scenery against the blue Pacific. Remember, other bikers and hikers, as well as 4WD trucks use these roads, so use caution and

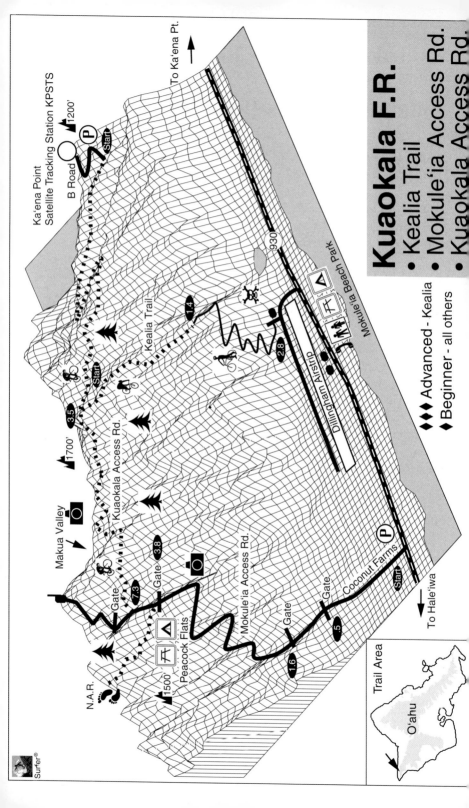

travel at speeds that are safe.

Beginner mountain bikers will find miles of 4WD roads that provide a relatively safe trip, due to its wide roads. Typical bumpy terrain with uphills and downhills give beginners a good sense of mauka trail riding. The more conservative riders can just follow the main road indicated by the arrow signs. Use your odometer and map to determine mileage.

Kuaokala Access Road serpentines through cool forests full of tropical birds and often has deep mud puddles under its overgrown trees. However, it is a long ride, and riders should prepare for a few hours minimum when riding out and back. No water is available on this long journey, so bring plenty with you.

The roads fork in different directions, so follow your map and the road most traveled. The Kealia Trail links with the main road and is the only single track for mountain bikes in this area.

The dirt road will eventually intersect with Mokule'ia Access Rd. Take a left and follow the paved road down and up to a locked gate. Peacock Flats campground is on your immediate right. A sheltered picnic table and one portable rest room is available for use. Camping is allowed by permit only.

Mokule'ia Access Road to Peacock Flats

How to get there: The Mokule'ia Access Road is located on O'ahu's scenic northwestern coast. Head north on Farrington Highway 930. Drive past Waialua High School and continue for two miles until you reach the first left at the coconut tree farm. Park on the right as you enter the access road. Do not leave valuables in the car which might provoke thieves.

As you proceed up this road, you will pass three gates which are usually locked. If they are open, do not attempt to drive a vehicle past them or your vehicle may be locked in.

Mokule'ia Access to Peacock Flats: 3.8 miles one way
Rating: Beginner to advanced
Special: No permit is necessary to use this access road. Camping at Peacock Flats or exiting via the Ka'ena Point Satellite Tracking Station road will require a permit from DLNR. See Permit Information.

Note: Paved road. Wet ride ok. The Pahole Reserve is a Natural Area Reserve NAR. No bikes on single track (see map).
Hazards: Livestock, occasional vehicular traffic and cliff areas.
Amenities: Camping, portable rest room and shelter.
History: *Mokuleʻia*, lit. "island of abundance".
Elevation Range: Sealevel to 1,500 feet

Start this ride in the cool of the morning or late afternoon as there is minimal shade. Bring plenty of water, sunscreen and a hat to protect yourself from the sun and heat. The Mokuleʻia Access Road is a paved road which travels up an arduous incline. If you can conquer this hill without a dismount, you are ready for anything.

The first mile from the parking lot is level with a mild uphill and is perfect for the training beginner rider. At the 2.2 mile mark, the uphill grade steepens, and riding becomes very slow and hot as it passes through cow pastures. If the physical demands of this ride don't take your breath away, the spectacular views of the North Shore certainly will. During the winter months from November to May, you may be able to see humpback whales off-shore.

Peacock Flats campground will be on your left at approximately 3.8 miles. You may follow the 4WD road on the left up another .5 mile to the Pahole Reserve boundary. Being a Natural Area Reserve, the hiking trail is off-limits to mountain bikes. If you leave your bike behind, the hike will take you to breathtaking view of Makua Valley on Oʻahu's western shoreline.

Follow the paved road another .80 mile to access the Kuaokala Access Road. This connects to the Kealia Trail and the Kaʻena Point Satellite Tracking Station. (see map)

Kealia Trail

How to get there: This technical trail is located above Dillingham Airfield in Mokule'ia on O'ahu's northwest coast. The Kealia Trail has a steep grade with loose terrain, so it is not ridable as an uphill.

For directions to connect to the Kealia Trail from above, refer to the map of Mokule'ia Access to Peacock Flats or Kuaokala F.R. Road (KPSTS).

Kealia Trail: 2.8 miles one way (Not including access routes. Add mileage from Peacock Flats or KPSTS)

Rating: Advanced

Special: No permit needed when accessed from the Mokule'ia Access Road. Permit only needed when using the KPSTS access. See Permit Information.

Note: 4WD and single track. DO NOT RIDE single track on wet or rainy days.

Hazards: Steep cliffs, loose and narrow terrain, roots and rocks.

Amenities: None

History: *Kealia*, lit. "salt encrustation".

Elevation Range: 1,700 feet to sealevel

The Kealia Trail is a fun and technical downhill ride. At about the .75 mark of the 4WD road, certain areas are rutted out due to rain and erosion. Be careful if you are going fast. Follow the road most traveled along the ridge top. At the end of the road you will find the beginning of the single track on your left, hidden in the ironwood forest. Now is the time to adjust those shocks and put them to the test. The next 1.4 miles is a bumpy switchback that harbors steep cliffs with loose rocks, drop-offs and various technical terrain. Use extreme caution and dismount when appropriate. Only competent advanced mountain bikers should challenge this trail.

This trail offers some fantastic views of the North Shore and Mokule'ia. Directly below the trail lies the Dillingham Airfield. This is the home of glider rides, aerobatic bi-planes and skydiving schools. While on the trail, you can sometimes see and hear the sailplanes flying low overhead. Sometimes, they fly so close, you can see their smiling faces.

Just off-shore, surfers ride waves during the winter season. The waves on this northern coastline get as big as 20 to 30 feet. Only a brave few ever take that challenge.

When you reach the bottom of the trail, you will pass the glider port. You may turn left at Farrington Highway 930 to Ka'ena Point or go right to the Mokule'ia Access Road.

Ka'ena Point Trail

How to get there: Located at the westernmost tip of O'ahu. Head west on Farrington Highway 930 in Mokule'ia to the end of the paved road. Park and lock your car, but do not leave valuables in the car.

Ka'ena Point: 5.0 miles one way
Rating: Beginner to advanced
Special: No permit is needed to enter the Ka'ena Point area. The roads and dunes near the lighthouse are part of a Natural Area Reserve NAR. This fragile coastal ecosystem consists of many endangered native Hawaiian plants and animals. Be extremely careful when entering into this area. Absolutely no bikes are allowed in the bird nesting area, as bikes frighten the nesting seabirds. Leave your bike outside the walking path (see map), and only enter on foot to view this native coastal ecosystem. Stay on the main trail. No pets allowed.
Note: 4WD road. Wet ride ok, however, beware of the clay-like mud which is hard to ride.
Hazards: The winter months bring dangerous high surf, so stay clear of areas exposed to breaking waves. Hikers are plentiful. Watch out for motorcycles, 4WD's, ATV's on the western side of the point.
Amenities: Showers and restrooms at Ka'ena State Beach Park
History: Also known as leina a ka'uhane, the "leaping place of souls". In ancient times, Hawaiians believed that souls of the dead leap off an area of this point into the land of dead.

An old railroad track, still visible in some areas, is from a time when trains were used to transport pineapple around the point. *Ka'ena*, lit. "the heat".
Elevation Range: Ocean level

It is recommended that you start this ride in the cool of the morning or late afternoon as there is very minimal shade. Bring plenty of water, sunscreen and a hat to protect yourself from the sun and heat.

Ka'ena is a visitors paradise and is known for its dry and beautiful setting along the blue Pacific. This semi-level bumpy road goes around the entire point and ends at Yokohama Beach on the west side.

As seen on your map, the Mokule'ia side of the point is a maze

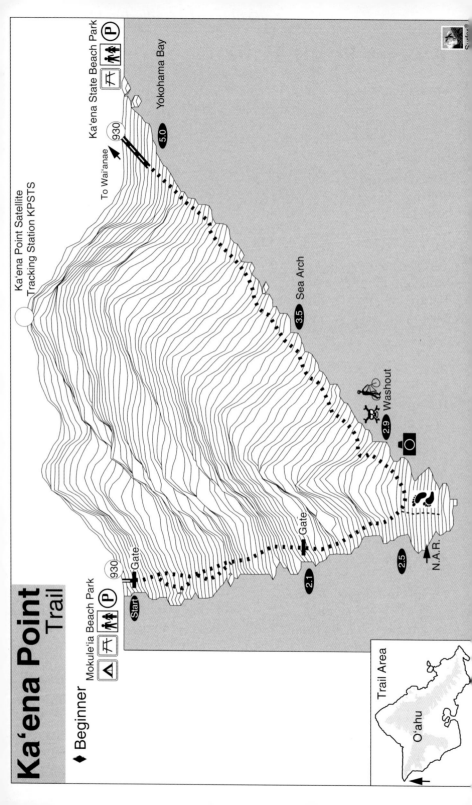

of dirt roads. The mauka road consists mainly of dirt and rock, while the makai road is mostly sand. If you are caught in the rain on this ride, try to take the makai road because it is more porous. The clay-like mud of the mauka road will quickly cake-up your tires and prevent tire rotation.

Beyond the gated boulder barricade lies the NAR. The clearly marked main trail will bring you around the point without disturbing this fragile ecosystem. If you want to view the protected area, keep your bike outside on the main trail and walk in via the sandy path. Stay on the main trail. The Laysan albatross' and the wedge-tailed shearwaters have their nesting grounds here, so don't take short-cuts or make your own path.

During the winter breeding season, generally November through May, Humpback whales are often seen breaching off the point. The endangered Hawaiian monk seals can also be sighted resting on the beaches. Only an estimated 1,000 are still surviving today. Take all the pictures you  desire, but do not disturb the wildlife by getting to close. Terns, red footed boobies, green sea turtles and spinner dolphins can sometimes be seen from this dry, wind-swept point.

Toward the Yokohama side, there is one area where the sea has completely eroded the trail, so be careful. You will need to dismount and carefully carry your bike across to continue.

Continue further and look for the small blow hole in the rocks on the right side. Follow the kiawe tree laced road a short distance to the end at Yokohama Beach. Showers and restrooms are available across from the beach. High surf and hidden reef are common at this beach, so use caution if swimming here.

Private Pastures

Some of the most incredible places to ride on Oʻahu are on private property. For this reason, detailed maps of these areas are not provided. Authorized access is required for your safety. If you choose to ride on private property, it is your responsibility to get permission and to obey their rules. Security personnel patrol these areas and can have you arrested for trespassing.

Mililani

How to get there: Head north on the H-2 freeway. Take the Ka Uka Blvd. exit #2 and turn right. Follow road down the Panaikauahi Gulch and back up the other side. Turn at the first right at the Waiawa Correctional Facility sign and proceed up the hill approximately 1.5 miles. Off the paved road, many dirt roads and trails disappear into the woods. Park on public roads and follow any of these for access to the riding trails.

Rating: Intermediate to advanced

Special: Permission is only granted to organized groups and clubs that provide releases and carry insurance. Contact Gentry Properties and Castle & Cooke Land Company. See Appendix for contact number.

Note: Wet ride ok. May be slippery and/or cake-like mud.

Amenities: None

History: *Mililani,* lit. "beloved place of chiefs".

Hazards: Recreational vehicles, roots, rocks, cliff areas and loose terrain.

Mililani has miles of 4WD roads and single tracks and is often used by 4WD's, motorcycles and ATV's. Use caution when you hear approaching motorized vehicles. Pull well off the road or trail and wait for them to pass.

You can ride for hours here and never see your own tracks. Mililani has seemingly endless single tracks and dirt roads with plenty of mud puddles. Remember where you came from so you don't get lost.

An all day ride will take you past incredible scenery and different terrain. Roots, rocks, and overgrown trees and bushes make Mililani a real challenge. Uphill leg burns and fast downhills, mixed with winding turns and tricky stream crossings are also common. A variety of tropical fruit can be found throughout your ride. Bring plenty of water and energy food. You'll definitely need it.

Kahuku (Waiale'e motorcycle track)

How to get there: Head north on Kamehameha Highway on O'ahu's North Shore. Pass the Sunset Beach Elementary School approximately 1.2 miles. On the mauka side of the highway, you will see a dirt road for the Kahuku Moto-X Track. Follow the dirt road up to the gate. Here you will need to pay an entry fee. Continue up the road until you reach the race track. Park your vehicle and beware of motorcycles.

Rating: Beginner to advanced
Special: Permit is not needed. However, a $5.00 fee per bike per day is required. Park is open from 8am-6pm weekends and federal holidays only.
Note: 4WD road and single track. Wet ride ok. May be slippery when wet and have cake-like mud.
Amenities: Camping and portable restrooms.
Hazards: Motorcycles, 4WD's, ATV's, cliffs, roots, rocks and loose terrain.
History: *Kahuku*, lit. "the projection". Site of frequent motorcycle and mountain bike racing.
Elevation Range: Sealevel to 900 feet

Located on O'ahu's scenic North Shore. The Kahuku Race Track is on state land that is leased by Hawai'i Motorsports Association. The track is primarily used for motorcycle racing and practice sessions on weekends and federal holidays. Mountain bikers should stay off the race track. Ride on the many 4WD roads and single tracks that comprise the Kahuku area. Yield to motorcycles at all times. Strict regulations regarding helmet use apply. DO NOT be caught with out your helmet on, or you will be asked to leave.

When you ride Kahuku, you are blessed with miles of perfect mountain bike roads and trails. Steep uphills and fast downhills with plenty of technical riding for trials riders. The forests consist of ironwood trees with dry twigs covering the ground. Be ready for fast and furious riding. Kahuku is a great ride for aggressive riders who just have to skid, slide, jump and make shortcuts. Once you visit Kahuku, rest assured, you'll be back. See Appendix for contact number.

Queen's Beach

How to get there: Proceed east on Kalaniana'ole Highway 72. Pass Sandy Beach Park approximately 1.5 miles. On the makai side of the road there is an undeveloped section of land opposite the Hawai'i Kai Golf Course. Park on the public roads well off the highway.

Rating: Beginner to advanced

Special: Permission is needed from the owner Bishop Estate or their lessee. See Appendix.

Note: 4WD and single track area. Wet ride ok. Prepare for hot and dry climate with minimal shade.

Amenities: Parking, swimming and fishing.

Hazards: Surf, rocky shoreline, loose terrain and recreational vehicles.

History: Former ranch land of Alan Davis. The Davis home was destroyed by a devastating tsunami in 1946. Some remnants may still exist.

Elevation Range: Ocean level

This entire area is currently private property and owned by Bishop Estate, however, the State of Hawai'i has plans to acquire it and make it a park. It offers approximately 20 acres of non-developed coastal property with perfect trails for beginner mountain bikers. The trails also provide a good test for your full suspension. The terrain consists of rocks, boulders, Whoop-D-Doos and a combination of dried dirt, wet mud and deep sand roads.

Fronting this land is a beautiful coastline. High surf is common along this shoreline, predominately during the summer. Use caution when riding near shoreline or when swimming. Queen's Beach bakes in the sun, so bring plenty of water and sunscreen. Certain areas may require a dismount because of steep drop-offs or loose gravel.

Bike Tours - O'ahu

If you're looking for a guided mountain bike tour through hidden O'ahu, then the following information is for you. Some of the best off-road rides are found on private property and are best accessed by taking a guided tour. The following tours offer incredible landscape and history and are found in the lush Ko'olau Mountains.

Bike Hawaii - Adventure Tours

Bike Hawaii, a division of 'Ohana Adventure Tours, offers full service bike and hike tours on the island of O'ahu.

The Ka'a'awa Valley Tour and the O'ahu Bike & Hike provide guests exciting interpretive tours for all skill levels. All Bike Hawaii tours include round-trip van transportation from Waikiki and include Bell helmets and front suspension Kona Mountain Bikes and Trek 800's.

Ka'a'awa Valley Tour:

Ka'a'awa Valley is located on O'ahu's northeastern shore. The 1,000 acre tropical valley is alive with a running stream and a variety of plants and animals, many of them indigenous to the Hawaiian Islands. Along the tour, you'll stop at various film sites from Godzilla to Jurassic Park, a military bunker converted into a movie museum and a recently constructed kauhale (small Hawaiian village).

Easy-to-ride dirt roads and challenging single track make this tour an excellent choice for all skill levels. Beginner riders will enjoy the many pasture roads with scenic backdrops while advanced riders can hone their skills on the available single track.

Scenic ocean views and sheer valley walls provide a stunning backdrop to this epic

valley ride. You may be able to snack on fresh (seasonal) island fruit picked from the overhanging trees as you ride. Just when you need it most, you'll pedal through a refreshing stream to cool you off.

This Bike Hawaii adventure ends with a delicious lunch where you'll be awarded a breath taking view of this historic Hawaiian valley from a shady pavilion.

See Appendix for contact number.

O'ahu Bike & Hike:

The O'ahu Bike & Hike is popular 5-mile downhill bike ride over lush paved jungle road and includes a guided hike to a beautiful cascading waterfall. Since the ride is over paved road, it is technically not mountain biking. However, this tour awards guests a pleasant downhill ride with fantastic views above Waikiki and Honolulu. Your friendly and knowledgeable guide will share interpretive information on Hawaii's flora, culture and geology. A quick group stop will allow for an unobscured photo opportunity, before continuing downhill.

After the ride, you'll be shuttled to the trailhead of a tropical valley hike along a stream. As you hike, you'll be relaxed by the sights and sounds of flowing streams and singing forest birds.

Capture the waterfall with your camera. Then, splash in to cool off in the natural rock pool surrounded by 'Ohi'a 'ai (mountain apple) and Mango trees. Use a provided mask and snorkel to view the native 'o'opu fish.

See Appendix for contact information.

O'ahu Explorer:

Bike Hawaii shares O'ahu with visitors from around the globe on their multi-day, multi-sport adventure in Ka'a'awa Valley. This historic verdant valley offers numerous mountain bike trails for all skill levels, from single track to pasture roads. Activities include hiking to a scenic overlook to capture Kane'ohe Bay from high above. Adventures include beach activities, like swimming and snorkeling. Kayaking, surfing, horseback riding, ropes course, atv and helicopter rides are also available to guests at additional costs.

Tours include Hawaiian games, a visit to a *kauhale* (Hawaiian

village), various film sites and a classic movie museum. Tent camp under the Hawaiian sky with Bike Hawaii. Includes ground transportation, meals and most of the gear. Trips are customized and offered with strict minimums by request only. See Appendix.

Club Rides

Hawai'i Bicycling League
Hawaii Mountain Bike Advisory Committee

The Hawai'i Bicycling League (HBL), founded in the 1960's, is a non-profit, organized group of dedicated bicycle enthusiasts on the island of O'ahu. Aside from being the largest bicycle advocate in the State of Hawai'i, HBL offers fun on and off-road rides to the public. Members of HBL receive the club publication *Spoke-n-Words* and reap the benefits of being a club member, including discounted inter-island bike travel aboard Hawaiian Airlines. Along with weekend treks, HBL hosts the Century Bike Ride, Hawai'i's largest bicycle event. Other HBL events include their Hale'iwa Metric Century, Tread Lightly (off-road) and the Rock Concert at Ka'ena Point (off-road). **The Hawai'i Mountain Bike Advisory Committee (HMBAC)**, HBL's dirt division, offers off-road trail rides on occasion when they are not conducting volunteer trail maintenance. For up-to-date information on group rides, events and trail work, contact HBL. See the Appendix for phone numbers.

Ko'olau Pedalers

Ko'olau Pedalers was founded in 1992 by a group of avid cyclists on O'ahu. This non-profit organization conducts on and off-road rides primarily on the beautiful windward side of the island. While promoting bicycle safety with informative tips on education, Ko'olau Pedalers meets almost weekly to enjoy group rides.

If gearing up and getting down to some fun riding interests you, contact Ko'olau Pedalers. See Appendix for contact numbers.

Kaua'i - The Garden Island

Kaua'i is the fourth largest of the Hawaiian Islands and is approximately 8 million years young. It is 33 miles long and 25 miles wide with 90 miles of pristine coastline. The highest peak is Kawaikini at 5,243 feet.

Kaua'i has some extraordinary geological features that are known worldwide. Probably the most famous of these is the "Grand Canyon of the Pacific", Waimea Canyon, 15 miles long and 3,400 feet deep. Neighboring Wai'ale'ale is the wettest spot on earth and has an average annual rainfall of over 451 inches. Known for the filming of the movie Jurassic Park, Kaua'i boasts beautiful valleys and hidden worlds of tropical splendor.

While on Kaua'i, enjoy some of the island's famous beaches: Polihale, Lumaha'i and Po'ipu are just a few of the many. With the scorching Hawaiian sun, tender foot malihini's may find the sand a breathtaking experience.

While others spend time at the beach, mountain bikers enjoy the thrill and action of pedaling some of the most scenic and inspirational mountainous trails the planet has to offer. As you crest the ridgeline of the Makaleha Mountains, or stop near the one of the many precipitous cliffs of the Waimea Canyon, you'll be in awe of an island that time forgot.

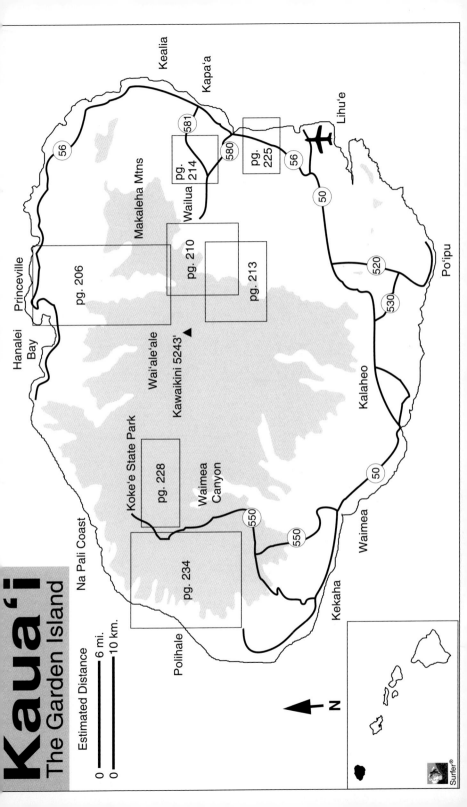

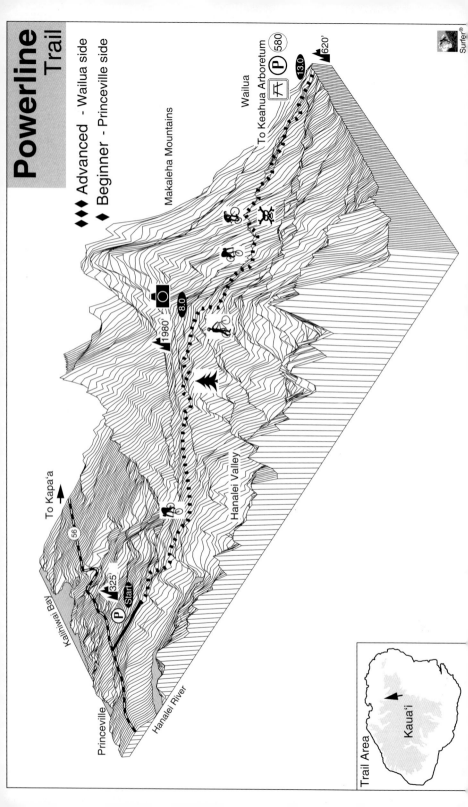

Powerline Trail

How to get there: Trail access is between the 27 and 28 mile markers along Kuhio Highway 56 on the northern coast of Kaua'i. Turn mauka at the Princeville Ranch sign (Kapa'ka Street) and proceed up approximately 1.7 miles to the dirt road marking the beginning of Princeville's Powerline Trail.

The trail can also be accessed from Wailua on the eastern side of the island. From Wailua, turn mauka onto Kuamo'o Road 580 and head up for six miles until you reach the Keahua Arboretum. Use caution when crossing the stream which flows across the road. Continue past the stream just .1 mile and you will find the Lihu'e Powerline Trail access on your right.

Powerline Trail: 13 miles one way
Rating: Beginner to intermediate from Princeville side
        Advanced from Wailua side
Special: No permit needed.
Note: Challenging 4WD road. Slippery when wet.
Hazards: Occasional vehicular traffic, hunters, deep mud, ruts, steep and loose terrain.
History: Used primarily as a service road for the electric company.
Elevation Range: 325 to 1,980 feet

Powerline Trail is an incredible ride which cuts the island almost in half. Starting from Wailua, Powerline is a grueling hillclimb. The trail starts at approximately 620 feet, and in just five miles, reaches an altitude of approximately 2,000 feet before descending into Hanalei Valley on the northern side of the island. The lush, tropical views of the native Hawaiian rainforest here confirm Kaua'i's nickname, "The Garden Island".

As you begin the climb, Kuilau Ridge is on your immediate right above the Keahua and Kawi streams which are fed by the Makaleha Mountains. On your left, commonly hiding in cloud cover, is Wai'ale'ale, the wettest spot on earth with an average of 451 inches of rainfall annually.

Proceeding further, the climb is impossible to ride in certain sections and will require carrying your bike. Even 4WD's have a hard time in these sections. At approximately 2.4 miles on your right will be a clear view of the Kapakaiki Falls which flow into the Keahua Stream below.

Once you crest Kualapa Ridge at approximately 5 miles, you will find a breathtaking view of Hanalei River which flows some 10 miles seaward to the beautiful Hanalei Bay. Looking behind you is an equally exceptional view of Wailua; Nounou Mountain "Sleeping Giant"; Kilohana Crater and the Makaleha Mountains. Spend some time here to relax, enjoy the scenery, and get your bearings. Geographically, you are in the heart of Kaua'i.

The ride down to Hanalei is a gradual eight mile ride over a variety of terrain. Again, some muddy or rutted sections are technical and may require you to dismount to safely pass.

For a more user friendly access, beginner and intermediate riders should access Powerline Trail from Princeville and turn around at the ridge top to avoid the steep and tricky route on the Wailua side.

Kuilau Ridge Trail

How to get there: Located on the eastern side of Kaua'i. From Wailua, turn mauka onto Kuamo'o Road 580 and head up for six miles. Kuilau Trail is on your right, just before you reach the Keahua Arboretum and stream crossing.

Kuilau Trail: 2.2 miles one way. Connecting with Moalepe Trail, makes an optional 9.5 miles out and back. See map.
Rating: Intermediate to advanced
Special: No permit needed. Stay on main trail. Do not ride when wet.
Note: Single track.
Hazards: Narrow path with steep cliffs and slippery sections.
Amenities: Shelter and tables on trail and at arboretum..
Elevation Range: 515 to 1,080 feet

The Kuilau Trail, an excellent ride for jungle lovers, offers a ride on the wild side. Twisting up Kuilau Ridge, the trail is narrow in some places, so you may have to get off and walk your bike in those tricky sections.

After the first mile through the thick canopy of trees, the vegetation opens up and provides stunning views. Across the valley on your left, you can see the Powerline Trail marked by power lines and utility poles. Behind them, the dark walls of Wai'ale'ale are shadowed almost year 'round by clouds and rain.

Just beyond the first mile, a picnic shelter and table are available to rest before continuing your ascent. Continuing further at 1.75 miles, you will cross a bridge above a stream. The bridge is slippery when wet. All around you is 'uluhe fern, kukui nut and guava trees. Enjoy the fresh guavas that are seasonally plentiful. You will enter an ironwood and paperbark forest and at 2.2 miles, the trail does a sharp u-turn to the right. This is the connecting point to the Moalepe Trail and ends the Kuilau Trail. Proceed down and refer to Moalepe Trail for what to expect.

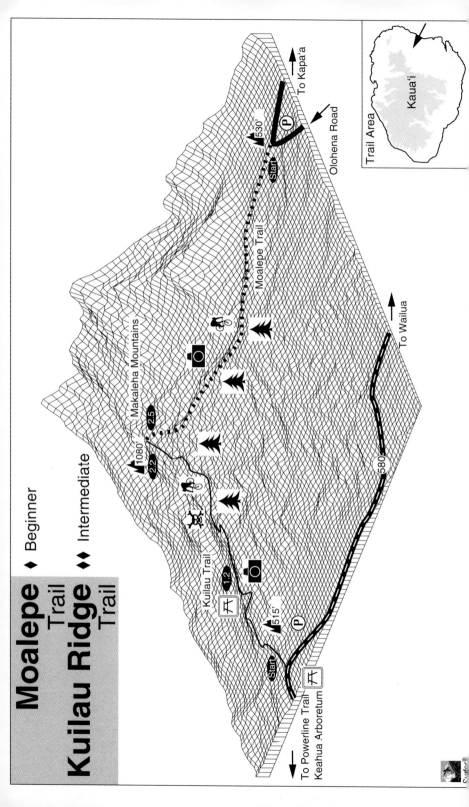

Moalepe Trail

How to get there: From Kuhio Highway 56 in Kapa'a on the east shore of Kaua'i, proceed mauka on Kuamo'o Road 580 for approximately 2.75 miles and turn right onto Kamalu Road 581. Drive to the end and turn left onto Olohena Road and continue up until you reach the trailhead at the end of the road.

Moalepe Trail: 2.5 miles one way. Connecting with Kuilau Trail, makes an optional 9.5 miles out and back.
Rating: Beginner to advanced
Special: No permit needed. Stay on main trail. Wet ride okay.
Note: Double track and 4WD road.
Hazards: Narrow path with cliffs and slippery sections. 4WD vehicles and horses are probable.
Amenities: None
History: *Moalepe*, Lit. "chicken comb".
Elevation Range: 530 to 1,080 feet

Starting from Olohena Road, Moalepe Trail offers a mild dirt road for the first 1.7 miles up and is ridable for beginners. Private ranch lands border the first portion of the road and are fenced off, so stay on main road. Excellent views of the Makaleha Mountains are found on your right.

The trail narrows and becomes muddy after 1.7 miles. Only intermediate to advanced riders should proceed from here. You may have to walk your bike around the tricky sections of this double track. Some mud puddles are deeper than they appear, so be ready for a dirty ride. Moalepe Trail intersects Kuilau Trail at the u-turn in the ironwood trees. You may continue down Kuilau for another 2.2 miles to the Keahua Arboretum. Here you can enjoy a refreshing swim in the stream. Refer to Kuilau Trail for information on what to expect.

Wailua Forest Management Road

How to get there: Located on the eastern side of Kaua'i. From Wailua, turn mauka onto Kuamo'o Road 580 and head straight up for approximately 6.2 miles until you reach the Keahua Arboretum. You may park here and continue straight along the unimproved road through multiple stream crossings. Follow the map.

Wailua Forest Management Road: 10.4 miles out and back
Rating: Beginner to advanced
Special: No permit needed.
Note: 4WD road. Wet ride okay.
Hazards: Slippery when wet. Occasional vehicular traffic. Ruts and potholes. Flashfloods may occur during periods of heavy rains. Do not cross streams if rain is heavy.
Amenities: Parking area, covered picnic tables and swimming at Keahua Arboretum. Picnic area also available 3 miles in.
History: Forest management road. Old access road to the sugar plantations.
Elevation Range: 515 to 1,130 feet

This ride begins at a popular swimming hole at Keahua Arboretum, a perfect beginning and end for your adventure through a lush forest reserve. Your biggest obstacles are the stream crossings. Cross slowly, and if the flow is to strong or deep to stand in, do not attempt the crossing. Wait it out until the water level subsides.

The unmaintained paved road enters the Waikoko Forest Reserve and turns into a gravel road just two miles beyond the arboretum. Here, you will need to turn right and proceed up through a forest of paperbark trees. This bumpy road has many intersecting roads, some of which lead to gauging stations. Stay on the road most traveled and use your map. At about 2.8 miles, you can make a left turn to rest at a picnic area approximately .2 mile in.

Continuing up the main road, a locked gate prohibits vehicles from passing further. From here, you may proceed around the gate for another mile to where the road ends just downstream from the base of Wai'ale'ale and Kawaikini, Kaua'i's highest mountain peak.

Be prepared for wet and muddy conditions along this entire ride. Finish your ride with an invigorating swim at the Keahua Arboretum.

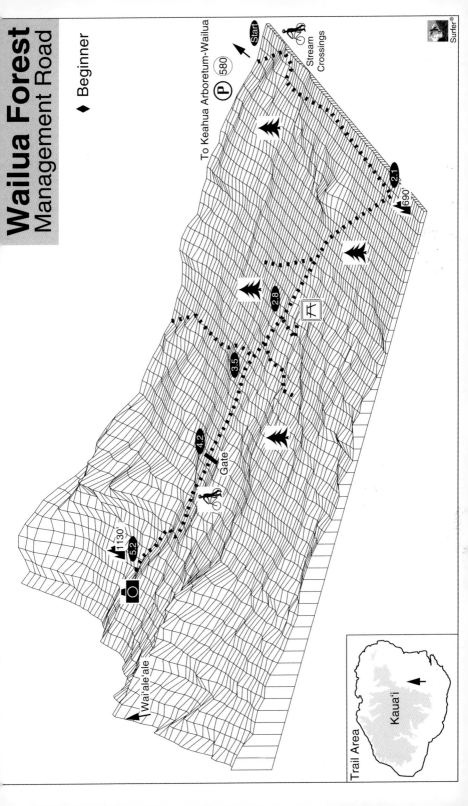

Kuamoʻo-Nounou Trail

◆ Intermediate

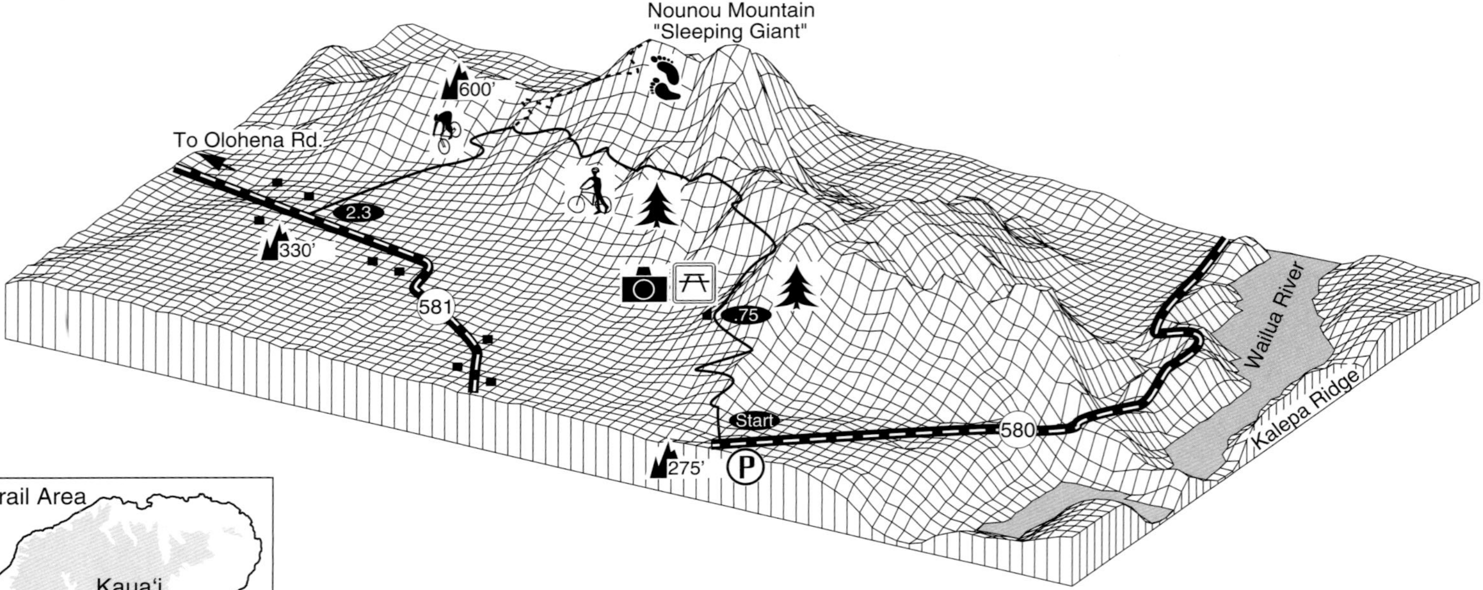

Nounou Mountain "Sleeping Giant"

Wailua River

Kalepa Ridge

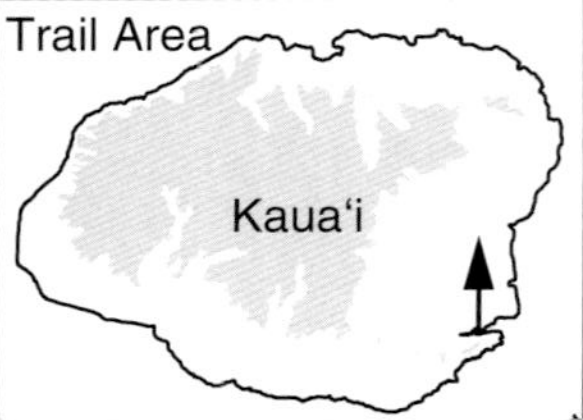

To Olohena Rd.

580

581

275'

330'

600

2.3

.75

Start

Trail Area

Kauaʻi

Surfer®

Kuamo'o-Nounou Trail

How to get there: From Kapa'a on Kaua'i's eastern shore, Turn mauka from Kuhio Highway 56 onto Kuamo'o Road 580 and head up approximately 2.3 miles until you reach the trail head on your right. Park here and continue up the trail.

Kuamo'o-Nounou Trail: 2.3 miles one way to Kamalu Road.
Rating: Intermediate to advanced
Special: No permit needed.
Note: Single track. Do not ride when wet or raining.
Hazards: Roots, rocks and cliff areas.
Amenities: Shelter and picnic table at .75 mile mark.
History: *Kuamo'o*, lit. "backbone". *Nounou*, lit. "throwing".
Elevation Range: 275 to 600 feet

The Kuamo'o-Nounou Trail is a quick and fun single track that wraps around the lower slopes of Nounou Mountain. Also known as the "Sleeping Giant" due to its profile from a distance, Nounou offers beautiful views up slope toward the Makaleha Mountains and Wai'ale'ale.

Beginning from Kuamo'o Road this tropical treat starts off by crossing a small bridge that rises immediately above Opaeka'a Stream. Just one mile downstream, Opaeka'a Falls is a popular tourist attraction. The trail continues and ascends to a shelter. Here is a clear view of Wailua Homesteads and its many farm homes and livestock. In the distance, the Makaleha Mountains stand tall against the gray cloud layer that typically hugs the summit walls. After even slight rains on the Makaleha Mountains, waterfalls appear as if they were pouring directly out of the sky.

Continuing further, winding in and out of the dense forest canopy, the trail is laced with roots making for fun and challenging obstacles. After entering the pine forest, the trail begins to lead downward. You will soon reach a fork in the trail. Stay left and continue down to the exit point at Kamalu Road 581. From here you can retrace your steps or proceed left onto Kamalu Road and left again onto Kuamo'o Road to your original starting position. See the map.

Kalepa Ridge Trail

How to get there: Heading towards Lihu'e from Kapa'a on Kaua'i's eastern shore, turn right onto Kuhio Highway 56 south. Heading up just .4 mile, turn right onto Hulei Road. Drive up .25 mile to end of road. Access is straight up the paved road with the cable across it. Approximately .5 mile up, a hair pin turn marks the trail head to the right.

Kalepa Ridge: 6 miles out and back
Rating: Intermediate to advanced
Special: Land locked forest reserve. Crosses private land to get to State trail. Stay on trail and do not enter the cane fields.
Note: Single track. Do not ride when wet.
Hazards: Narrow trail with ruts, cliffs, roots and rocks.
Amenities: None
History: Feral cattle destroyed much of the ridge vegetation during the mid-1900's. Trail was later used for reforestation attempts. *Kalepa*, lit. "trade".
Elevation Range: 250 to 720 feet

After reaching the Kalepa Ridge trail head, follow the trail to the east for unforgettable views of Kaua'i's eastern shoreline and mountainous backdrops. From many sections of this trail, you will have a flawless 360° view which includes the coastline, the Makaleha and Nounou Mountains; in the distance to the south, Kipu Ridge; and to the west Kilohana Crater and Wai'ale'ale.

Kalepa Ridge has a series of ups and downs, some of which may be to steep to ride. Certain drop-off sections will also require you to dismount and carry your bike. At approximately 1.8 miles, you will reach the bottom of a fun and challenging downhill. From here, the trail continues up the ridge as more of a hiking trail. Hard core riders can proceed with bikes in hand until the trail becomes ridable again.

Continuing north along the ridge top, the trail ends overlooking the famous Wailua River. Across the valley to the north, you can see Opaeka'a Falls, just below Nounou Mountain. Spend a few moments to rest and enjoy the scenery before returning along the ridge.

The scenic Waimea Canyon State Park.

Advanced riders descend rugged single track.

The view from Kalepa Ridge above Wailua River.

Princeville side of Powerline Trail.

Droppin' in.

The edge of the world. Waimea Canyon.

Deep valleys along the Na Pali Coastline.

Misty clouds embrace mountain riders. *Kalalau Valley.*

Pristine coastline near Kealia.

The view of Polihale from Kauhao Ridge.

Hanalei sunset from the Princeville side of the Powerline Trail.

Powerline Trail.

The steep descent to Wailua, Powerline Trail.

Road side near Waimea Canyon State Park.

Kauhao Ridge Road.

Off the beaten path. Mohihi.

Kalepa Ridge
Trail

♦♦ Intermediate

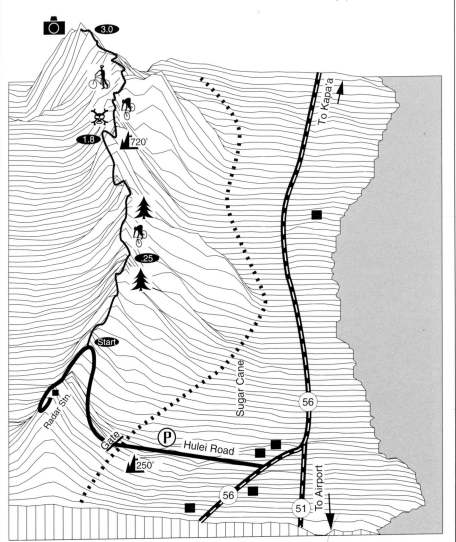

3.0

1.8

720'

.25

To Kapa'a

Sugar Cane

Start

Radar Stn.

Gate

P Hulei Road

250'

56

56

51

To Airport

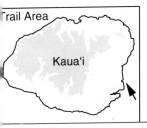

Trail Area

Kaua'i

Surfer®

Koke'e State Park

How to get there: Located in the mountains of northwest Kaua'i. From Kaumuali'i Highway 50, turn mauka on Waimea Canyon Drive 550 or Koke'e Road 550. Both of these roads connect and lead you to Koke'e State Park some 18 miles up. Proceed up the steep, winding paved road until you the reach Koke'e Lodge on your left just beyond the 15 mile marker.

Koke'e State Park is Kaua'i's pride and joy. Immense tree lines, lush forest reserve and a variety of native Hawaiian birds are common sights here. Along the right side of upper Koke'e Road is the world famous Waimea Canyon. Also known as, the "Grand Canyon of the Pacific", Waimea's steep canyon walls are as deep as 3,400 feet in some places. Eroded from nearly six million years of water run off, these red clay cliffs are a picture perfect backdrop for the lush green landscapes and cascading waterfalls that pour into the winding rivers on the canyon floor below.

Hawaiian nene geese of Koke'e State Park.

From the top of Koke'e Road, Pu'u o Kila Lookout provides an incredible view of picture perfect Kalalau Valley and the crystal blue Pacific Ocean. Up here, the forest is alive with rare native birds, such as the nene goose, 'elepaio, and the 'apapane. The world's largest dragonflies (*pinao*) also make Koke'e their island home.

At the Koke'e Lodge, hot meals and delicious island coffee are available at nominal prices. Visit the Koke'e Natural History Museum and educate yourself on the different species of plant life in this area by taking a short .25 mile nature hike around the backside of the museum. Free plant guides are available in the museum.

Koke'e State Park borders Waimea Canyon State Park, Na Pali - Kona, Ku'ia Natural Area, Alaka'i Wilderness and Pu'u Ka Pele

Forest Reserve. There are many hiking trails within these areas, however, for the protection of many native species, mountain bikes are required to stay on the 4WD roads only.

The ridge roads begin in the lush forests of Koke'e and Waimea Canyon State Park and descend into the lower elevations of Na Pali-Kona and the Pu'u Ka Pele Forest Reserve above Kaua'i's dry western coastline. Often times riders will come across pigs, black-tailed deer and wild goats. From many vantage points riders will see the private island of Ni'ihau, just twenty miles across the Kaulakahi Channel. In the late afternoon, you can catch unforgettable sunsets with colors ranging from brilliant orange to pastel blues and pinks. If you're lucky, you might even see the green flash.

Within Koke'e State Park, numerous camping sites are available, but by permit only. Twelve cabins are available at reasonable rates, but need to be reserved well in advance. The cabins are furnished with refrigerators, stoves, hot showers, linen, and cooking utensils. For further information, refer to the Appendix for Kaua'i. Remember to dress accordingly, at 3,000 to 4,000 feet, the weather can be cold and wet.

Mohihi - Camp 10 Road

How to get there: Just beyond the 15 mile marker on Koke'e Road, access Kumuwela Road directly across from Koke'e Lodge. You may also use the Mohihi Road access, further up 550. Use your map.

Mohihi- Camp 10 Road: 6 miles one way
Rating: Beginner to advanced
Special: Permits only needed to camp. Stay on main road, no biking on hiking trails.
Note: Dirt road with potholes.
Hazards: Vehicular traffic, horses, hunters, extremely slippery when wet, stream crossings should be waited out during strong flows, steep sections, roots, rocks and cliff areas.
Amenities: Camping grounds, parking and shelters.
History: Old access road to maintain the ditch systems which provide water to the sugar plantations below in Kekaha.
Elevation Range: 3,500 to 3,700 feet

One ride to the end of Mohihi - Camp 10 Road and you'll be sure to come back for more. Mohihi provides riders countless turns and a series of wild up and downhills, definitely a thorough work-

Mohihi - Camp 10 Road

Beginner

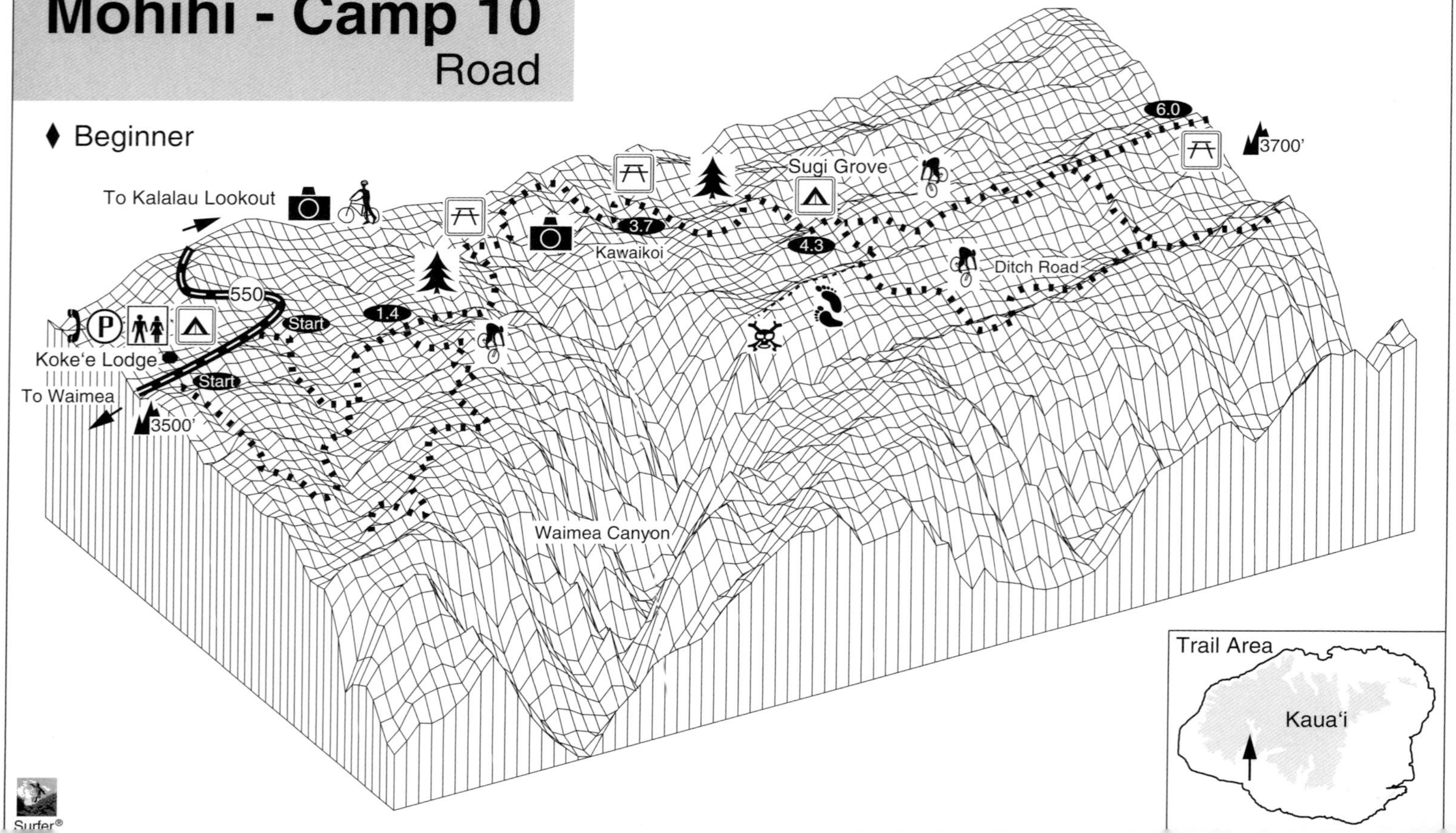

Trail Area

Kaua'i

To Kalalau Lookout

Koke'e Lodge

To Waimea

550

Start

Start

3500'

1.4

Kawaikoi

3.7

Sugi Grove

4.3

Ditch Road

Waimea Canyon

6.0

3700'

Surfer®

out. After even a slight rain, the hard packed dirt road can become slick as ice. Go slow or walk your bike down the steep gradients when wet.

Along this heavenly ride, many hiking trails venture off into the wilderness. All hiking trails are off-limits to bicycles. You must come back another day and hike by foot to enjoy the rest of this pristine area.

The scent of fresh ginger often fills the air. Quiet and relaxing sounds of the bubbling streams also add to the beauty of this six mile ride. Near your third mile, stop at the Alaka'i picnic area on the right. A small shelter and table provides sweeping views of the world famous Waimea Canyon.

Proceed further to Sugi Grove. Often frequented by campers, Sugi Grove is situated on the bank of Kawaikoi Stream. Introduced in the 1930's, many sugi pine (Japanese cedar) and California redwood trees flourish here. For a truly magical experience, continue

up further another .5 mile and turn right onto the intersecting dirt road. Ride less than a mile in where the ridge offers spectacular views of the canyon from a different perspective. A foot trail to the right brings adventurous hikers to the edge of precipitous cliffs well over 2,000 feet above the canyon floor. Hike it at your own risk.

Proceeding to the end of Mohihi, another shelter with a picnic table may be used to rest before returning. Seasonal blackberries can be picked fresh along the ride back. Take your time and enjoy the ride. Camping is recommended to get the full effect of this tropical wilderness. Capture the sights on film, for this ride is truly a ride through the Garden Island.

Miloli'i Ridge Road

How to get there: Proceed up Koke'e Road and just before the 14 mile marker, turn left onto Makaha Ridge Road. Follow the paved road down approximately .5 mile and access to Miloli'i Ridge will be on your right.

Miloli'i Ridge: Approximately 10.7 miles round trip
Rating: Intermediate to advanced
Special: Steep road. Endurance and stamina required.
Note: 4WD road.
Hazards: Vehicular traffic, steep and tricky sections, loose surface, roots, rocks ruts and cliffs.
Amenities: None
History: Old access road used for reforestation. *Miloli'i*, lit. "fine twist".
Elevation Range: 3,400 to 2,000 feet

Get ready to ramble. Miloli'i Ridge offers some of the wildest downhill fun through forests of native acacia koa trees, past a variety of pine, and ends up with an incredible view of the blue Pacific. Fast sections of dirt road keep you on the edge of your seat while carefully negotiating the downhill road. Some rutted sections and other tricky areas come up fast, so use caution and travel at speeds that are safe. During your ride, you might see black-tailed deer, pigs and goats wandering the treacherous valleys and cliffs.

Once you've reached the end of the road, a breath taking view of the ocean and Miloli'i Valley are to the right. Typically, this area is quiet, allowing you to here the shreak of white tailed tropicbirds, the cry of mountain goats and the occasional laugh of the erckel francolin. Behind you to your right is Pa'aiki Valley. The small beach at Miloli'i is also visible from atop this near 2,000 foot perch. Down on the ocean, tour boats cut across the dark blue ocean with their white wakes. Bring a camera and enjoy the view. The ride back up will require stamina and a whole lot of of water.

Kauhao Ridge Road

How to get there: Just beyond the 13 mile marker on Koke'e Road, turn left and proceed straight on the dirt road. At approximately .3 mile in, pass the Methodist Camp and turn right at the dirt road. Another .35 mile in, stay right where the Contour Road intersects with Kauhao Ridge Road.

Kauhao Ridge Road: Approximately 8 miles out and back
Rating: Intermediate to advanced
Special: No permit needed.
Note: 4WD road.
Hazards: Slippery when wet. Ruts and fallen tree debris are common.
Amenities: None
History: *Kauhao*, lit. "the scooping".
Elevation Range: 3,500 to 1,800 feet

While many ridge roads in this area are difficult, Kauhao Ridge Road provides a medium grade and is not as steep as Miloli'i, but provides plenty of fast trackin', downhill fun. You may encounter an occasional 4WD, so use caution on the blind turns, and don't exceed safe speeds.

In certain sections, you will catch glimpses of the blue ocean in the distance contrasting with the green foliage and red dirt road. Descending further down the road through the eucalyptus forest, many vista points afford views of the panoramic scenery. On your right across Kauhao Valley is Makaha Ridge. To the left is Ka'aweiki Valley.

Continue to the end of the road to find a foot path which leads out to an overlook of the long stretch of beach at Polihale State Park on Kaua'i's west shore. Across the Kaulakahi Channel is the forbidden island of Ni'ihau. Privately owned by the Robinson family, only invited guests are allowed to visit. The smaller islet just north of Ni'ihau is called Lehua.

Inviting as it may seem, there are no mountain bike trails to the beach from here. So, relax and enjoy a PowerBar before the ride back up.

Ka'aweiki Ridge Road

How to get there: Follow the directions to Kauhao, but turn left at the Contour Road and make your next right onto Ka'aweiki. See map.

Ka'aweiki Ridge Road: Approximately 7 miles out and back.
Rating: Intermediate to advanced
Special: No permit needed. Stay on main road.
Note: 4WD road.
Hazards: Slippery when wet. Ruts and fallen tree debris are common. 4WD vehicles.
Amenities: None
History: *Ka'aweiki*, lit. "tie a little"
Elevation Range: 3,500 to 2,000 feet

Pass the open gate at the entrance to Ka'aweiki. From here the dirt road curves down through forest reserve over a mild to medium downhill slope. Vehicular traffic may be present. Ruts, branches and other obstacles should also be anticipated.

When possible, stop and listen to the wind through the trees and the distant sound of streams in the valley. Pull off the road and catch a glimpse of Ka'aweiki Valley to the right and Hikimoe to the left. Hikimoe translates to mean "resting place". A good idea before beginning the pedal back up.

The end of the Ka'aweiki Road offers visitors a view of the white sandy coastline of Polihale Beach, two thousand feet below. Across the Kaulakahi Channel, is the island of Ni'ihau and the smaller islet Lehua, both approximately 20 miles away.

Take a rest, but be sure to save enough water for the ride back up. Have fun!

Polihale Ridge Road

How to get there: Heading up Koke'e Road 550, turn left at the second dirt road past the 12 mile marker. Road should be clearly marked with a sign indicating Polihale Ridge Road.

Polihale Ridge Road: 9 miles out and back from Koke'e Road
Rating: Intermediate to advanced
Special: No permit needed. Stay on main road.
Note: 4WD road.
Hazards: Slippery when wet. Ruts and fallen tree debris are common. 4WD vehicles.
Amenities: None
History: *Polihale*, lit. "house bosom"
Elevation Range: 3,500 to 1,400 feet

From Koke'e Road 550, go one mile on the dirt access road until it intersects with the Contour Road. Continue straight across the Contour Road to access Polihale Ridge Road. From here, it's a fun 3.5 mile downhill before reaching the steep cliffs above Polihale Beach on Kaua'i's western shoreline.

Expect a medium grade with occasional obstacles such as ruts and fallen branches. As you proceed down the road, you will pass through forests of native koa and introduced Norfolk pine and ironwood trees. The surface of the road is often covered with pine cones. Use caution when riding over this loose debris. Stay on the main road and don't attempt any animal trails worn by feral pigs and black-tailed deer.

Through clearings in the trees, you can see the red dirt road winding ahead on the ridge top. The view to your right is of Hikimoe Valley and to the left is Ha'ele'ele Valley. At approximately 3.2 miles, the road forks. Either way is fine. The road ends shortly with spectacular views of the ocean below. In the winter when the waves are up, you can hear the surf breaking on the coast below. Enjoy a relaxing stay.

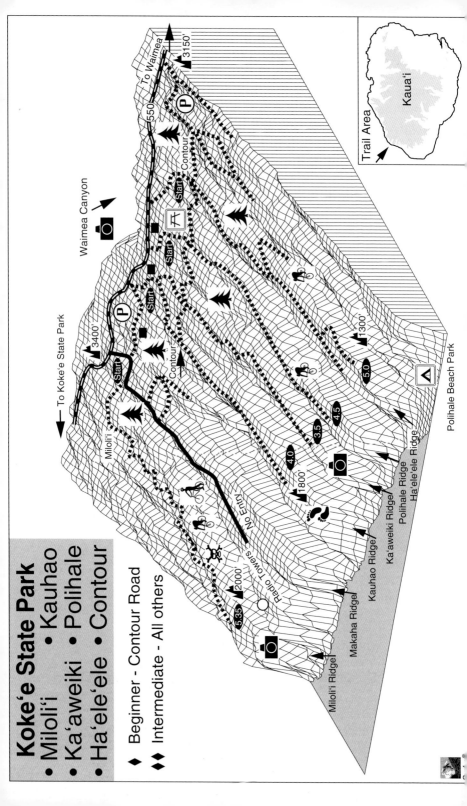

Ha'ele'ele Ridge Road

How to get there: From the 12 mile marker on Koke'e Road 550, turn left at the Ha'ele'ele Ridge Road sign. Follow the winding dirt road 1.5 miles. Pass the Lua Reservoir to the Contour Road intersection. Proceed straight across to Ha'ele'ele Ridge Road.

Ha'ele'ele Ridge Road: 10 miles out and back from Highway 550
Rating: Intermediate to advanced
Special: No permit needed. Stay on main road.
Note: 4WD road.
Hazards: Slippery when wet. Ruts and fallen tree debris are common. 4WD vehicles.
Amenities: None
History: *Ha'ele'ele*, lit. "blackish"
Elevation Range: 3,150 to 1,300 feet

Ha'ele'ele Ridge provides riders with a hard pack, red dirt road that winds under the tall eucalyptus and Norfolk pine trees of the Pu'u Ka Pele Forest Reserve. As with all the roads in this area, even a slight rain will make the red clay surface slippery, which may cause quick unexpected falls.

An enjoyable ride for both full suspension and rigid frame riders, Ha'ele'ele is smooth in some sections and rutted and rooty in others. Continue down approximately 2 miles from the Contour Road and you will see a left turn. This is an optional route that will lead you down a 1.5 mile dirt road to what is known as Kepapa Spring. Don't expect a fountain of youth or even a pleasant swimming hole.

Further down Ha'ele'ele Ridge Road, rugged and rocky sections make up the last half mile before reaching a short single track overlooking Polihale Beach and the Pacific Missile Range Facility (PMRF). To the left is the mouth of Ka'ula'ula Valley.

Have fun and enjoy the view before heading back up.

Contour Road

How to get there: Access to the Contour Road is gained just beyond the 11 mile marker on the left while heading up Koke'e Road 550. Park your car well off the road. See map.

Contour Road: 6.5 miles one way
Rating: Beginner to advanced
Special: No permit needed. Stay on main road.
Note: 4WD road.
Hazards: Slippery when wet. Ruts and fallen tree debris are common. 4WD vehicles.
Amenities: Shelter with picnic tables and restroom.
History: Connector road to the various ridge roads.
Elevation Range: 2,800 to 3,500 feet

Contour Road is a dirt road which runs parallel to Koke'e Road 550 and connects all five of the lower ridge roads. This fun ride provides an off-road experience through a variety of timberline forest. A small picnic area is located at approximately 2.5 miles in on the right. Riders of all skill levels can enjoy this ride over a mildly bumpy red dirt road. Riders can expect a series of mild up and down hills.

Intermediate riders will enjoy a faster pace, but are urged to use caution in blind corners due to occasional hikers and vehicles. Some

mud puddles may exist. Remember that even with a slight rain, the surface may become as slick as ice. Go slow when wet and have fun.

If you have the energy, it is a rigorous ride down and back up the many connecting ridge roads. Magnificent viewpoints overlooking the western coast of Kaua'i are found at the base of any of these ridge roads.

Private Pastures
Kealia Trails

How to get there: Located approximately one and a half miles north of Kapa'a town is Kealia Beach. Turn right into the beach park between the 9 and 10 mile mark and follow the unkept pothole road which continues north along the coast. From here, many alternate dirt roads and single track can be found through the ironwood pine trees and sugar cane fields on your left.

Kealia Trails: Approximately 4 miles one way to Anahola
Rating: Beginner to advanced
Special: Private property of AMFAC Sugar. Contact field manager at (808) 245-7325 for up to date access information and permission.
Note: Single track and dirt roads cross. Use caution when wet.
Hazards: Motorcycles, 4WD's, cliffs, roots and rocks.
Amenities: Beach access
History: Area is still in use for growing sugar cane by AMFAC Sugar. The end of the road comes out at Anahola and crosses Department of Hawaiian Home Lands. *Kealia*, lit. "salt encrustation".
Elevation Range: Sea level to 100 feet

Kealia is a mild grade ride which offers riders a variety of single track and 4WD roads. Less than half a mile from Kealia Beach Park, riders find trail access on the left. A slight hill climb brings you to the start of the many trails. Some tricky sections may require riders to dismount and walk their bikes. In some sections, the marks of skilled and veteran riders have been left behind showing their preferred line to clear the various obstacles.

Along the ride you will come across many intersecting trails and roads which open up to beautiful views of the coast. The first beach you come to after Kealia is known as Donkey Beach. Riders often stop here for a swim. Swimmers should use caution during large surf and be aware of occasional Portuguese Man-Of-War jelly fish which blow in from the ocean.

After exploring the many different trails and coastal views, riders will end up at Anahola, a small village and beach park some four miles away. The last section before Anahola is private property of Department of Hawaiian Homelands DHHL. When these signs are spotted, it is recommended to detour and head back along the coastal trails. DHHL should be contacted for authorization to cross their land.

Bike Tours - Kaua'i

Bike Hawaii - "Kaua'i Explorer"

Bike Hawaii's "Kaua'i Explorer" includes overnight stays in stylish mountain cabins with showers, electricity, kitchen and warm beds to sleep in. Day trips include, mountain biking dirt road and/or single track with optional paved road routes, hiking treks to remote wilderness areas, kayaking scenic fresh water rivers and visiting small villages and native communities of the Garden Isle. Explore Kaua'i with Bike Hawaii's "Kaua'i Explorer". Trips are customized and offered with strict minimums by request only. Contact information is in the Appendix.

Kaua'i Adventure Trek

Kaua'i Adventure Trek offers easy, fun mountain biking on old sugar cane dirt roads through Kaua'i's arid south/western coastline. With stops at old sugar mills and a short tunnel ride, you'll get a taste of old Hawai'i. A short 20-minute hike will lead you to a secluded beach for rest and relaxation.
Gear, helmets and lunch included. See Appendix for contact numbers.

Koke'e Downhill

If you enjoy the thrill of coasting down a paved road from a lush tropical rainforest, then check out Kaua'i Coasters or Outfitters Kaua'i.. They both offer organized bike tours complete with bikes, helmets, gloves, jackets and a van ride up the hill. Guests enjoy a continental style breakfast and island narrative by their knowledgeable guides. Riders gear up at the Waimea Canyon Lookout at approximately 3,000 feet. After a short safety briefing, riders follow the group leader down the 12 mile winding road to sea level in Kekaha.

This tour is not designed for speed. Rather, riders enjoy a relaxing descent from Koke'e with unforgettable views of Waimea Canyon on the left and the green landscapes of sugar cane fields on the right.

For riders of all skill levels with a sense of adventure, enjoy a day of coastin' with Kaua'i Coasters or Outfitter's Kaua'i.
See Appendix for contact numbers.

Appendix

Hawai'i

Permit Information

Hawai'i Volcanoes National Park (808) 985-6000
PO Box 52
Hawai'i Volcanoes National Park, HI. 96718
* 24 Hour Volcano Eruption update
* Camping available at Namakani Paio and Kamoamoa

Volcano House (808) 967-7321
P.O. Box 53
Hawai'i Volcanoes National Park, HI. 96718
* Lodging or cabins by reservation only

Kilauea Military Camp KMC (808) 967-8333
Armed Forces Recreation Center
Attn: Reservations Office
Hawai'i Volcanoes National Park, HI. 96718
* Cabins for use by active and retired military personnel

Department of Land and Natural Resources (808) 974-4221
Division of Forestry and Wildlife
19 East Kawili Street
Hilo, HI. 96720
* Na Ala Hele - statewide trails and access (808) 974-4217
* Tent and cabin permits for
Keanakolu, 'Ainapo and Waimanu

Hawai'i State Parks (808) 974-6200
75 Aupuni Street #204
Hilo, HI. 96720
* Tent and cabin camping permits for
Kalopa and Mackenzie State Parks
Hapuna Beach and Mauna Kea State Parks

County Parks (808) 961-8311
Dept. of Parks and Recreation
101 Pauahi Street #6
Hilo, HI. 96720
* Camping and picnic permits for county parks
Kolekole, Laupahoehoe, Spencer, Mahukona, Kapa'a and Keokea,
Ho'okena, Miloli'i, Whittington, Punalu'u and Issac Hale Beach
Parks

Mauna Kea Summit Weather Information (808) 974-4203
Mauna Kea Visitor Information Station (808) 961-2180

Bike Tours (companies in bold conduct off-road tours)

Bike Hawaii (808) 734-4214/(877) MTB-RIDE (see article pg. 97)
(Custom multi-day only)
PO Box 240170
Honolulu, HI. 96824
email: tours@bikehawaii.com
website: www.bikehawaii.com

Mauna Kea Mountain Bikes (808) 883-0130 (888) MTB-TOUR
(see article pg. 97)
PO Box 44672
Kamuela, HI. 96743
email: mtbtour@aol.com
website: www.bikehawaii.com/maunakea

Kona Coast Cycling (808) 327-1133
74-5588 Bldg. G4, Pawai Pl.
Kailua-Kona, HI. 96740
email: bikeinfo@cyclekona.com

Paniolo Adventures (808) 889 5354
Mile 13.2 Kohala Mountain Road (Hwy 250)
PO Box 44327
Kawaihae, HI. 96743
website: www.panioloadventures.com

Adventure Tours (808) 966-4968
PO Box 182
Pahoa, HI. 96778

Red Sail Sports (808) 885-2876 Waikoloa

South Point Bicycles (808) 929-8559/7613

Backroads (800) GO-ACTIVE

Big Island Mountain Bike Association BIMBA (see Bike Clubs)

Bike Shops

Hilo Bike Hub (808) 961-4452
318 East Kawili Street
Hilo, HI. 96720
email: hilobike@lava.net
* Sales/Service/Rentals

C&S (808) 885-5005
64-1066 Mamalahoa Highway
Kamuela, HI. 96743
email: cands11111@aol.com
* Sales/Service/Rentals

B&L Bike and Sport (808) 329-3309
75-5699 Kopiko Place
Kailua-Kona, HI. 96740
website: www.blbikes.com
* Sales/Service/Rentals

MidPacific Wheels (808) 935-6211
1133-C Manono Street
Hilo, HI. 96720
* Sales/Service .

Hawaiian Pedals (808) 329-2294
75-5744 Ali'i Drive
Kailua-Kona, HI. 96740
website: www.hawaiianpedals.com
* Sales/Service/Rentals

HP BikeWorks (808) 326-2453
74-5599 Luhia Street
Kailua-Kona, HI. 96740
email: teamhp@gte.net
website: www.hpbikeworks.com
* Sales/Service/Rentals

Dave's Bike & Triathlon (808) 329-4522
75-5669 Alii Drive
Kailua-Kona, HI. 96740
* Sales/Service/Rentals

Bike Clubs & Environmental Groups

Big Island Mountain Bike Association BIMBA (808) 961-4452
PO Box 6819
Hilo, HI. 96720-8934
website: www.interpac.net/~mtbike/

Hawai'i Cycling Club
PO Box 3246
Kailua-Kona, HI. 96745
website: www.hawaiicyclingclub.com

PATH - Peoples Advocacy for Trails Hawai'i (808) 967-8603
PO Box 62
Kailua-Kona, HI. 96745
website: www.hialoha.com/Path/

WOMBATS-Women of Mtn Biking and Tea Society (808) 967-7569
Fung Irvine
PO Box 327
Volcano, HI. 96785
website: www.wombats.org

Maui

Permit Information

Department of Land and Natural Resources
Division of Forestry and Wildlife (808) 984-8100
54 South High Street #101
Wailuku, HI. 96793
* Na Ala Hele - statewide trails and access (808) 873-3508
(for Maui, Moloka'i and Lana'i)
* Volunteer Trail Work Program (808) 871-2521
* Game Management (808) 871-4210
* Natural Area Reserves System (808) 871-2620

Hawai'i State Parks (808) 984-8109
54 South High Street #101
Wailuku, HI. 96793
* Camping permits for
Polipoli And Wainapanapa State Parks

County Parks (808) 270-7389
Dept. of Parks and Recreation
War Memorial Gym
1580 Ka'ahumanu Avenue
Wailuku, HI. 96793
* Camping and picnic permits for
Baldwin and Kanaha Beach Parks

Mount Haleakala Summit Report (808) 572-4400

Bike Tours

Bike Hawaii (808) 734-4214/(877) MTB-RIDE
(Custom multi-day only)
PO Box 240170
Honolulu, HI. 96824
email: tours@bikehawaii.com
website: www.bikehawaii.com

Maui Mountain Cruisers (808) 871-6014/(800) 232-6284 (see pg. 121)
PO Box 1356
Makawao, HI. 96768
website: www.mauimountaincruisers.com

Maui Downhill (808) 871-2155/(800) 535-BIKE
199 Dairy Road
Kahului, HI. 96732
website: www.mauidownhill.net

Aloha Bicycle Tours (808) 249-0911/(800) 749-1564
PO Box 455
Kula, HI.96790
website: www.maui.net/~bikemaui

Haleakala Bike Company (808) 575-9575/(888) 922-2453
810 Haiku Rd. Suite 120
Haiku, HI. 96708
email: staff@bikemaui.com
website: www.bikemaui.com

Emerald Island (808) 573-1278/(800) 565-6615
website: www.mauibiking.com

Hawaii Downhill (808) 893-2332
520 Keolani
Kahului, HI. 96732

Mountain Riders (808) 242-9739
222 Lalo St.
Kahului, HI. 96732
website: www.mountainriders.com

Upcountry Cycles (808) 573-2888/(800) 373-1678
website: www.maui.net/~wayner

Bike Shops

The Island Biker (808) 877-7744
Hawaiian Island Center
415 Dairy Road
Kahului, HI. 96732
email: rjn@maui.net
website: www.islandbiker.com
* Sales/Service/Rentals

Haleakala Bike Company (808) 572-2200
810 Haiku Road #120
Haiku, HI. 96708
email: staff@bikemaui.com
website: www.bikemaui.com
* Sales/Service/Rentals/Tours

South Maui Bicycles (808) 874-0068
1993 #5 South Kihei Road
Kihei, HI. 96753
email: hackett@maui.net
* Sales/Service/Rentals

West Maui Cycles (808) 661-9005
840 Wainee C-5
Lahaina, HI. 96761
email: wmcycles@maui.net
* Sales/Service/Rentals

Extreme Sports Maui (808) 871-7954
360 Papa Place #F
Kahului, HI. 96732
email: extreme@maui.net
website: www.extremesportsmaui.com
* Sales/Service/Rentals

Bike Clubs

Maui Mountain Bike Club
PO Box 689
Makawao, HI. 96768

Moloka'i

Permit Information

Department of Land and Natural Resources
Division of Forestry and Wildlife (808) 984-8100
54 South High Street #101
Wailuku, HI. 96793
* Na Ala Hele - statewide trails and access (808) 873-3508
* Camping permits for Waikolu Lookout

Hawai'i State Parks (808) 984-8109
54 South High Street
Wailuku, HI. 96793
* Camping permits for Pala'au State Park

County Parks (808) 553-3204
Dept. of Parks and Recreation
PO Box 526
Kaunakakai, HI. 96748
* Camping and picnic permits for
One Ali'i and Papohaku Beach Parks

Moloka'i Visitors Association (808) 553-3876 or (800) 800-6367
PO Box 960
Kaunakakai, HI. 96748

Bike Tours (companies in bold conduct off-road tours)

Moloka'i Ranch Outfitters Center (877) 726-4656 or (808) 552-2791 (see pg. 128)
PO Box 259
Maunaloa, HI. 96770
website: www.molokai-ranch.com

Moloka'i Bicycle (808) 553-5740 or (800) 709-BIKE
PO Box 379
Kaunakakai, HI. 96748
website: www.bikehawaii.com/molokaibicycle

Molokai Outdoor Activities (877) 553-4477
HC 01 Box 28
Kaunakakai, HI. 96748
website: www.molokai-outdoors.com

Bike Shops

Moloka'i Bicycle (808) 553-5740 or (800) 709-BIKE
PO Box 379
Kaunakakai, HI. 96748
* Sales/Service/Rentals /Tours
website: www.molokaibicycle.com

Lana'i

Permit Information

The Lana'i Company, Inc. (808) 565-3000
PO Box 630310
Lana'i City, HI. 96763

Department of Land and Natural Resources
Division of Forestry and Wildlife (808) 984-8100
54 South High Street #101
Wailuku, HI. 96793
* Na Ala Hele - statewide trails and access (808) 873-3508

Weather Information (808) 565-6033

Bike Tours (companies in bold conduct off-road tours)

Adventure Lana'i Eco-Center 808-565-7373 (see article pg. 151)
P.O. Box 63-1394 Lana'i City, HI 96763
email: trekmaui@maui.net
website: www.adventurelanai.com

Bike Rentals

Adventure Lana'i Eco-Center 808-565-7373
website: www.adventurelanai.com

The Lodge at Ko'ele (808) 565-7300
PO Box 630310
Lana'i City, HI. 96763

O'ahu

Permit Information

Department of Land and Natural Resources
Division of Forestry and Wildlife (808) 587-0058
1151 Punchbowl #224
Honolulu, HI. 96813
* Na Ala Hele - statewide trail and access program (808) 973-9782
* Natural Area Reserves System (NARS) Information (808) 587-0054
  native Hawaiian plant and animal protection

Department of Land and Natural Resources
Division of Forestry and Wildlife (808) 587-0166
1151 Punchbowl #325
Honolulu, HI. 96813
* Ka'ena Point Satellite Tracking Station access road (KPSTS)
* camping and picnic permits to Peacock Flats

Hawai'i State Parks (808) 587-0300
1151 Punchbowl Street #131
Honolulu, HI. 96813
* camping and picnic permits for
Sand Island, Kahana, Malaekahana and Keaiwa parks

County Parks (808) 523-4525
Dept. of Parks and Recreation
650 S. King St. Ground floor
Honolulu, HI. 96813
* camping and picnic permits for
Bellows, Hau'ula, Kahe Point, Kaiaka, Keaau, Kualoa, Mokule'ia, Nanakuli, Swanzy and Waimanalo Beach Parks

Private Property Access Contacts

Gentry Properties (808) 599-8366
* Mililani (Waiawa/Waipi'o)

Castle and Cooke Land Company (808) 548-4811
* Mililani

Hawai'i Motorsports Assn. race info. (808) 239-BIKE
P.O. Box 1654
Honolulu, HI. 96806
* Kahuku motor-cross track

Bishop Estate (808) 523-6200
567 South King Street
Honolulu, HI. 96813
* Queens Beach area

Bike Tours (companies in bold conduct off-road tours)
Bike Hawaii (808) 734-4214/(877) MTB-RIDE (see article pg.199)
PO Box 240170
Honolulu, HI. 96824
email: tours@bikehawaii.com
website: www.bikehawaii.com

Waimea Valley & Adventure Park (808) 638-8511
59-864 Kamehameha Highway
Hale'iwa, HI. 96712
website: www.atlantisadventures.com

Hawai'i Bicycling League HBL (see Bike Clubs)

Ko'olau Pedalers (see Bike Clubs)

Bike Shops
Barnfield's Raging Isle Sports (808) 637-7707
66-250 Kamehameha Highway Bldg. B
Hale'iwa, HI. 96712
email: ragingislebikes@hawaii.rr.com
* Sales/Service/Rentals

Bikefactory Sportshop (808) 596-8844
740 Ala Moana Blvd.
Honolulu, HI. 96813
email: bikefactory@hawaii.rr.com
website: www.bikehawaii.com/bikefactory
* Sales/Service

BikeWerx (808) 627-0714
95-1249 Meheula Pkwy. D-7
Mililani, HI. 96789
email: info@bikewerx.net
website: www.bikewerx.net
* Sales/Service

Eki Cyclery (808) 847-2005
1603 Dillingham Boulevard
Honolulu, HI. 96817
email: eki@aloha.com
website: www.ekicyclery.com
* Sales/Service

Island Triathlon and Bike (808) 732-7227
569 Kapahulu Avenue
Honolulu, HI. 96816
email: itb@aloha.net
website: www.trybikes.com
* Sales/Service/Rentals

The Bike Shop (808) 596-0588
1149 South King Street
Honolulu, HI. 96814
email: info@BikeShopHawaii.com
website: www.bikeshophawaii.com
* Sales/Service/Rentals/Tours

McCully Bike Shop (808) 955-6329
2124 South King Street
Honolulu, HI. 96826
email: customerservice@mccullybike.com
website: www.mccullybike.com
* Sales/Service

Gary's Bike World (808) 679-BIKE
94-910 Moloalo Street
Waipahu, HI. 96797
email: bikeinfo@garysbikeworld.com
website: www.garysbikeworld.com
* Sales/Service

Bike Clubs & Environmental Groups

Hawai'i Bicycling League (HBL) (808) 735-5756
Hawai'i Mountain Bike Advisory Committee (HMBAC)
3442 Wai'alae Avenue, Suite 1
Honolulu, HI. 96816
website: www.hbl.org
* group rides on/off road
* trail restoration
* bike education

Ko'olau Pedalers
PO Box 290
25 Kane'ohe Bay Dr. #106
Kailua, HI. 96734
* club rides

Sierra Club Hawai'i Chapter (808) 538-6616
PO Box 2577
Honolulu, HI. 96803
* hikes
* trail clearing and construction

Hawaiian Trail & Mountain Club
PO Box 2238
Honolulu, HI. 96804
* hikes
* trail maintenance

Hawai'i Nature Center (808) 955-0100
2131 Makiki Heights Dr.
Honolulu, HI. 96822
* environmental education for kids
* guided interpretive hikes
* adult classes

The Nature Conservancy (808) 537-4508
1116 Smith St.#201
Honolulu, HI. 96817
* land & environmental protection
* hikes

Hawai'i Visitors and Convention Bureau (808) 923-1811
2270 Kalakaua Avenue #801
Honolulu, HI. 96815
website: www.gohawaii.com

O'ahu Visitors Bureau (877) 525-OAHU
733 Bishop Street Suite 1872
Honolulu, HI. 96813
website: www.visit-oahu.com

Hawai'i Ecotourism Association (808) 235-5431
PO Box 61435
Honolulu, HI. 96822
website: www.hawaiiecotourism.org

Kaua'i

Permit Information

Department of Land and Natural Resources
Division of Forestry and Wildlife (808) 274-3433
3060 'Eiwa Street, Rm 306
Lihu'e, HI. 96766
* Na Ala Hele - statewide trails and access

Hawai'i State Parks (808) 274-3444
3060 'Eiwa Street, Rm 306
Lihu'e, Hawai'i 96766
* Camping permits for
Polihale, Koke'e, Hanakapi'ai, Kalalau and Miloli'i

County Parks (808) 241-6660
Dept. of Parks and Recreation
4444 Rice Street #150
Lihu'e, HI. 96766
* Camping permits for
Ha'ena, 'Anini, Hanalei, Anahola, Hanama'ulu, Lucy Wright and Salt
Pond Beach Parks

Private Property Access Contacts

AMFAC Sugar - Kaua'i (808) 245-7325
* Kealia Trails

Bike Tours (companies in bold conduct off-road tours)

Bike Hawaii (808) 734-4214/(877) MTB-RIDE (see article pg. 238)
(Custom multi-day only)
PO Box 240170
Honolulu, HI. 96824
email: tours@bikehawaii.com
website: www.bikehawaii.com

Bicycle Downhill (808) 742-7421 (see article pg. 238)
Kaua'i Outfitters Center
2827-A Poipu Rd.
Poipu, HI. 96756
website: www.outfitterskauai.com

Kaua'i Adventure Trek (800) 452-1113 (see article pg. 238)
1702 Haleukana St.
Lihue, HI. 96766
website: www.kauaiadventuretrek.com

Kaua'i Coasters (808) 639-2412 (see article pg. 238)
PO Box 3038
Lihu'e, HI. 96766
email: coast@aloha.net

Bike Shops
The Bike Doktor (808) 826-7799
5052 Kuhio Highway
Hanalei, HI. 96714
email: makani@aloha.net
* Sales/Service/Rentals/Tours

Bicycle John (808) 245-7579
3215 Kuhio Highway #7
Lihu'e, HI. 96766
website: www.bicyclejohn.com
* Sales/Service

Outfitters Kaua'i (808) 742-9667
2827-A Poipu Rd.
Poipu, HI. 96756
email: info@outfitterskauai.com
website: www.outfitterskauai.com
* Sales/Service/Rentals/Tours

Kaua'i Cycle and Tours (808) 821-2115
1379 Kuhio Highway
Kapa'a, HI. 96746
email: jbarth@aloha.net
website: www.bikehawaii.com/kauaicycle
* Sales/Service/Rentals

Bike Clubs
Kaua'i Bicycling Association
3215 Kuhio Highway #7
Lihu'e, HI. 96766

Kaua'i Bicycle Club
5052 Kuhio Highway
Hanalei, HI. 96714

Out-of-State Organizations

International Mountain Bike Association (IMBA) (303) 545-9011
PO Box 7578
Boulder, CO. 80306
website: www.imba.org
* mountain bike advocates

National Off-Road Bicycling Association (NORBA) (719) 578-4717
One Olympic Plaza
Colorado Springs, CO. 80909
* race directors
* insured events
* race licenses

Travel Accommodations

Inter-Island Travel

Aloha Airlines see local listings or (800) 367-5250 from mainland
Hawaiian Airlines see local listings/(800) 367-5320 from mainland
Expeditions Ferry (800) 695-2624

Rent-A-Car Companies

Dollar Rent-A-Car (800) 800-4000
Budget (800) 527-0700
Hertz (800) 654-3011
Avis (800) 321-3712
National (800) 227-7368
Alamo (800) 327-9633

Major Hotels

Outrigger Hotels & Resorts (800) 462-6262
Ala Moana Hotel (800) 367-6025
Sheraton Hotels (800) 325-3535
Hilton Hotels (800) 445-8667
Best Western (800) 528-1234
Aston Hotels (800) 321-2558

Alternative accommodations

Hawai'i
Outrigger Hotels (800) 462-6262
Volcano House (808) 967-7321 Hawai'i Volcanoes National Park
Carson's Volcano Cottage 808-967-7683/800-845-LAVA
Kilauea Volcano Kabins - 808-967-7773
Volcano Teapot Cottage - 808-967-8058/7112
Hale Ohia Cottage 808-967-7986/800-455-3803
Lokahi Lodge 808-985-8647/800-457-6924
Volcano Accommodations 808-967-8662/800-733-3839
Hale Kilauea 808-967-7591Volcano
Kona Coast B&B 808-323-2276/800-545-4390
Patey's Place 808-326-7018/800-972-7408 Kona
Arnott's Lodge -808-969-7097 Hilo

Moloka'i
Pu'u o Hoku Lodge (808) 558-8109 Halawa
Moloka'i Ranch (808) 552-2681 (800) 254-8871 Maunaloa
Pau Hana Inn (808) 553-5342 (800) 423-6656 Kaunakakai
Hotel Moloka'i (808) 553-5347 (800) 423-6656 Kaunakakai
Kaluakoi Resort & Golf (808) 552-2555 (800) 777-1700 Kaluakoi

Lana'i
The Lodge at Ko'ele (808) 565-7300 Lana'i City
Manele Bay Resort (808) 565-7700 Manele
Hotel Lana'i (808) 565-7211 Lana'i City
Sugarpine Vacation Rental (800) 943-0989 Lana'i City
Adventure Lana'i Eco-Center (808) 565-7373 Lana'i City

Maui
Outrigger Hotels & Resorts (800) 462-6262
Old Lahaina House (808) 667-4663 Lahaina
Lanikai Farm (808) 572-1111 Haiku
Garden Gate (808) 661-8800 Lahaina

O'ahu
Outrigger Hotels & Resorts (800) 462-6262
Hawai'i Backpackers (808) 638-7838 Hale'iwa
Island Hostel (808) 942-8748 Waikiki

Ali'i Bluffs Bed & Breakfast (808) 235-1124 Kane'ohe
Breck'n Packers Hawaiian Hostel (808) 638-7873 Sunset Beach
Hawaiian Seaside Hostel (808) 924-3306 Waikiki
Waikiki Hostel & Hotel (808) 924-2636 Waikiki

Kaua'i
Outrigger Hotels & Resorts (800) 462-6262
Princeville Resort (808) 826-4400
Hyatt (800) 233-1234
Koke'e Lodge- cabin rentals (808) 335-6061
Hale Le'a Cottage (808) 826-9105 Hanalei

References

Atlas of Hawai'i - Dept. of Geography University of Hawai'i. 1983
Arrigoni, Edward. *A nature walk to Ka'ena Point*
Bryan's Sectional Maps of O'ahu - EMIC Graphics, 1995
Cahill, Emmett. *The Shipmans of East Hawai'i*
DLNR's *Trail Inventory*
Girnani-Smith, Ruth. *The essential guide to O'ahu* 1988
Hawai'i's Birds - by Hawai'i Audubon Society
HBL's *Spoke-n-Words* monthly bicycle publication
Hiking Map & Guide Hawai'i Volcanoes National Park - Earthwalk Press 1992
IMBA's *Trail Development and Construction for mountain biking* and the *Educational Package.*
Nishida, Gordon., Tenorio, Joann. W*hat bit me?*
Prat, H. Douglas. *Enjoying birds in Hawai'i*
Pukui, Mary K., Elbert, Samuel H., and Mookini, Esther T. *New Pocket Hawaiian Dictionary* 1992 and *Place Names of Hawai'i 1974*
Sterling, Elspeth. Summers, Catherine *Sites of O'ahu* 1978.

Glossary

'Aina - Land.

Ahupua'a - Hawaiian land division that usually extended from mauka to makai.

Aloha - Hello, love, goodbye.

Boardwalk - An elevated walkway made of wood or synthetic planks tied together, preventing further deterioration of the heavily impacted trail below.

Bunny hop - A maneuver performed by placing both feet on the pedals and firmly grasping the handle bars, and with an upward motion, elevate your entire bike while riding without using a jump source.

Dab - Touching the ground or any solid object with your arms, body or feet to regain balance when riding.

DHHL - Department of Hawaiian Home Lands

Dismount - To get off the bike. Riders should dismount to safely pass a difficult or unridable section of trail.

DLNR - Department of Land and Natural Resources

DOFAW - Division of Forestry and Wildlife

Drop-off - A ledge or section of trail with significant variations in height. Small cliff.

Elevation range: The estimated elevations of the trail from lowest to highest.

'Ewa - O'ahu direction: towards the west. Also means bent.

4WD - Four wheel drive vehicle.

GMA - Game Management Area. Hunting area managed by the State of Hawai'i. Use caution in these areas. Stay on main trail.

Granny gear - the lowest gear on your bike. Enabling easier pedaling on steep uphills.

Heiau - Place of worship.

Kapu - Keep out. No trespassing.

Kiawe - A common tree found in lower dryer elevations that has small branches with sharp, hard wood thorns. Punctures bicycle tires easily.

KPSTS - Ka'ena Point Satellite Tracking Station.

Mahalo - Thank you.

Makai - Direction: towards the ocean.

Mauka - Direction: towards the mountain.

Na Ala Hele - "Trails To Go On," a. State trail and access program under the Department of Land and Natural Resources, Forestry and Wildlife

NARS - Natural Area Reserves System. A native species protection area.

Off-camber: A section of trail that is excessively uneven, usually angled towards a cliff.

'Ohana - Family

Ono - Good tasting. Also, type of fish.

Out and back - A trail requiring riders to return to their starting point along the same path. Not a loop.

Paniolo - Hawaiian cowboy

Pau - Finished

Pu'u - Hill, mountain, cone or peak.

Single track - A narrow dirt path cut through raw vegetation consisting of uneven terrain and natural obstacles.

Skid - The sliding action of a non-rotating tire when the bike is moving forward.

Switchback - A trail that zig-zags up or down a mountainside.

Trails - Single track or 4WD roads. Unpaved roads.

Trials - A style of riding that includes negotiating difficult and technical terrain without "dabbing".

Waterbars - Cut logs or other planking that is strategically placed diagonally across s trail and partially imbedded into the soil. They help control erosion by rerouting water run off.

Wheelie - Pedaling or pulling up hard enough to lift the front wheel off the ground while riding.

Whoop-D-Doo's - A series of large dips in a road.

The Author

Name: John Alford
Birthplace: Honolulu, Hawaiʻi
Occupation: Author, Bike Hawaii - President/Guide and EMT
Years mountain biking: Began riding the trails of Oʻahu in 1975 on a Schwinn Sting Ray and a Yamaha full suspension bicycle. During 1989 - 1991, won 1st place in a Novice - stage race, a Sport - criterium and an Expert - trials event on Oʻahu. In 1998, took 2nd place Sport - Hawaiʻi State Downhill Championships on Oʻahu.
Best biking experience: Mountain biking single track with fragrant Ginger blossoms surrounding the trail and a misty rainbow touching down at trails end.

Worst biking experience: Riding in traffic.
Type of riding: Recreational cross country, downhill and trials.
Favorite trails: Open ones. Single track preferred
Least favorite trails: Closed or paved trails
Hobbies: Founding member of HMBAC. Hawaiʻi State IMBA Representative. Also, volunteers to help restore and maintain trails with the State Division of Forestry and Wildlife - Na Ala Hele. Closet guitarist.

The Bike

Frame: Kona® Stinky Five - full suspension 7005 aluminum **Fork:** Marzocchi QR20 Z3 **Rims:** SunRims/DitchWitch **Tires:** Tioga **Brakes:** Hayes® Hydraulic Disc **Drive train:** Shimano XTR

The Accessories

Computer: CatEye® CC AT-100 (w/altimeter) **Lighting System:** Night Sun® Max - dual beam halogen 45 watts **Hydration System:** Camelbak® Blowfish 100oz **Helmet:** Bell - Psycho Pro® **Eye protection:** Oakley® **Chainring protection:** Rock Ring® **Nutrition Bars:** PowerBar®

Bike Hawaii shares the many hidden wonders of these tropical islands with visitors from around the globe. Experience lush, verdant valleys, waterfalls and streams, arid coastlines and sandy beaches.
Enjoy easy-to-ride dirt or paved roads.
Challenge the many miles of single track.
Bike Hawaii and learn Hawaiian culture, geology, flora and fauna.

Adventure tours for the adventure minded!

BIKE HAWAII

www.BikeHawaii.com
PO Box 240170
Honolulu, Hawaii 96824
toll free 877-MTB-RIDE

OUTRIGGER'S PACIFIC

We've earned the title "island experts" through our commitment to creating authentic experiences at each property, in every locale.

Select from 20 first class and deluxe hotels and resort condominiums in Hawaii, Fiji, Australia, Guam, and the Marshall Islands. Most offer ocean-front locations.

Call your travel agent or **1-800-OUTRIGGER** (688-7444). **outrigger.com**

OUTRIGGER®
HOTELS · RESORTS

Order Form

Name_____

Address_____

City_____ State_____ Zip Code_____

Email_____

Item	Qty./ Price	Shipping	Total

Mountain Biking the Hawaiian Islands $15.95 *FREE $_____
Second Edition

Bike Hawaii t-shirt..(specify size s, m, l, xl)..$20.00 $3.95 $_____
(4-color back. Design seen below)

                          Total payable $_____

*Free shipping allow 4 weeks delivery - USA only.
Add $3.95 for 2-day US Priority Mail
Add $7.00 shipping fee for orders outside the USA.

Please make check or money order payable to:
Bike Hawaii
P.O. Box 240170
Honolulu, Hawai'i 96824-0170
toll free 877-MTB-RIDE
email: john@bikehawaii.com
www.bikehawaii.com